Fly-Casting Fundamentals

Lefty Kreh

photographs by Jay Nichols

STACKPOLE
BOOKS

Published by
STACKPOLE BOOKS
5067 Ritter Road
Mechanicsburg, PA 17055
www.stackpolebooks.com

Printed in China

First edition

10 9 8 7 6 5 4 3 2 1

Library of Congress Cataloging-in-Publication Data

Kreh, Lefty.
    Fly-casting fundamentals / Lefty Kreh ; photographs by Jay Nichols.
        p.   cm.
    Includes index.
    ISBN-13: 978-0-8117-0565-3 (pbk.)
    ISBN-10: 0-8117-0565-X (pbk.)
    1. Fly casting.   2. Fly fishing.   I. Title.
SH454.2.K698   2012
799.12'4—dc23
                                                                    2011021077

Contents

Preface

Casting with Lefty Kreh, published in 2008, contains approximately 80,000 words and 1,100 photos. It was the most ambitious and most comprehensive casting book that I have ever written, and it took over two years to shoot the casting sequences and write the text. I am very proud of that book.

This book, *Fly-Casting Fundamentals*, distills the core principles and casts that I covered in detail in *Casting with Lefty Kreh.* By not including some of the more advanced and specialty casts, this is a much more affordable, streamlined manual of fly casting for entry-level fly fishers and other students of casting. And for casting instructors, I chose to include many of the teaching tips and casting aids that I have found helpful over the years.

With this book, I am confident that fly fishers can learn the casts that I consider essential for fresh and salt water.

Acknowledgments

So many people made this book possible. Joe Brooks got me started by giving me my first casting lesson. Countless friends and guides taught me various fishing casts. I consider Ed Jaworowski to be one of the best casting instructors in the world and we have learned so much from each other in our many discussions of casting and fishing. Oddly enough, after fly casting and fishing for more than sixty years I am still learning.

No one made this book possible more than Jay Nichols, a fine caster who took the photos, offered advice, and edited the manuscript.

I am indebted to Judith Schnell who encouraged me to do this book and to Amy Lerner, who helped make sense of the many photos.

CHAPTER 1

Principles and Other Key Concepts

Good casting is easy. I don't mean that it comes easily—it doesn't. It requires a lot of hard work, practice, and time on the water fishing. What I mean is that good casters expend very little effort making most casts. My main goal in this book is to show you how to cast—whether you are young or old, male or female—without exerting any more effort than is necessary.

If you watch several of the best baseball hitters, each has a different stance and holds the bat differently when up at the plate. But despite these individual styles, all baseball hitters are captive to certain principles of hitting. To hit a home run, they swing the bat through a long stroke; to bunt, they use a short stroke. It is the same with casting. We, too, are captive to basic principles, and if we don't adhere to them, our casting and fishing success suffers.

I realized in the late 1970s that people are built differently and fishing situations vary, so I stopped teaching the popular method of casting and began to teach basic principles. These are not my principles, they are physics. Once you understand these fundamental fly-casting laws of physics, you can improve your cast, adjust casting strokes to your physical makeup, or adapt them to a specific fishing situation.

There is no one way or style of casting simply because anglers are physically different, fishing situations vary, and many kinds of tackle and flies are used. You shouldn't cast a dry fly the way you would a weighted Clouser Minnow or a sink-tip line. The casting problems on a small trout stream, a big steelhead river, and a windy saltwater flat are so different that a single method or style of fly casting simply won't work in all situations. A good caster has the ability to make efficient casts under a wide variety of conditions and with a range of tackle—from light trout rods to tarpon rods. In this book I hope to not only help you improve your fly casting, but also help you better understand fly-casting mechanics and how to adapt them to various fishing conditions.

The best casters expend very little energy making most casts. Watching a young, strong caster huff and puff to send a fly line 100 feet doesn't impress me. What I look for, and take great pleasure in watching, is someone who casts well with as little energy as possible.

The Principles

All sports have principles that you must follow, but individual athletes accomplish their tasks in different ways. In fly casting (and other types of casting as well), we must abide by four basic principles—fundamental truths about casting—even though we have different needs and purposes. As individuals, we are physically different. Even among people who weigh the same, one person may have longer arms or be more powerfully built. Fly fishermen seek a huge variety of species under vastly different conditions. One angler fishes a narrow mountain brook and uses a tiny 2-weight rod and a delicate line to present a small Parachute Adams to a wary brook trout in shallow, air-clear water. Standing at the stern of a rocking offshore cruiser might be another fly fisherman throwing at a sailfish or marlin. Another angler may offer a huge Dahlberg Diver to a husky jungle peacock bass, while a steelhead fisherman will be casting a long two-handed rod and a pattern with bead-chain eyes a great distance across a big British

Columbia river. Waist deep in the surf, yet another fly fisherman bucks the stiff breeze casting a weighted line and a heavy fly to striped bass.

Because of these differences, no one method of fly casting is correct. Recognizing this in the late 1970s, I gave up teaching fly casting using conventional muscular movements and instead began to teach principles students could adapt for their physical makeups. Later they would be able to use these same principles to solve fishing problems and challenges as they arose. The advantages of the four principles are that you can adapt them to your physical build (no two people can really cast exactly alike), you can adapt them to your fishing situation, and you can analyze and correct your own cast. These principles are not based on particular motions, because not everyone can make the same motions. You should never cast the way your instructor casts. You should cast the way that suits your physical makeup.

Principle 1

You must get the end of the fly line moving before you can make a back or forward cast.

To get the end of the fly line moving, you need to remove all the slack from the line. If your line is not completely straight in front of you, some of your lifting motion is used to pull the line straight before the end starts moving. If you are trying to teach this principle to someone, simply place a garden hose on the lawn and put a single wave in it to resemble a potential sag in your backcast. Pick up one end of the garden hose and begin walking while looking at the other end of the hose. You won't move the far end of the hose until the large curve has been removed.

Pulling out the slack in your cast is wasted effort, and if you cast before you remove all the slack from the line and get the line end moving (drifting in the current doesn't count), you lose some of the benefits of accelerating the rod, and shock waves may develop in the line.

Moving Line

This sequence not only illustrates principle 1, but it is also handy for when you need to quickly cast as much as 20 feet of line and leader on the water without stripping in the line. Loose line lies on the surface in front of you, often after you have just replaced your fly. Once you move the end of the fly line in wide figure-eight loops, you can make the cast. Lower the rod tip close to the surface, and move the rod widely to the side. Never stop the rod as it sweeps back and forth.

Sweep the rod tip in the opposite direction. Don't make short sweeps or the line may tangle.

As the line moves toward the rod, elevate it.

Without stopping, sweep the tip in the opposite direction while keeping the rod tip high.

Immediately return the rod in the opposite direction while lowering the rod slightly to prepare for the best possible backcast.

Repeat the rod sweeping motion. The rod should never stop moving until the backcast.

Watch the line end while sweeping the rod back and forth. Anytime the line end begins moving, you can make the backcast in the direction opposite the target. Allow the backcast to almost straighten before starting the forward cast.

Principle 2

Once the line is moving, the only way to load the rod is to move the casting hand at an ever-increasing speed and then bring it to a quick stop.

A good casting stroke begins slowly, but smoothly and decisively, gradually accelerating to an abrupt stop. This long acceleration, followed by a speed-up-and-stop, occurs on both the back and forward casts. The sudden stop at the end of the cast is often called a power stroke, but applying "power" can spoil the cast. Instead of applying that find of force, at the end of the acceleration, briefly move the rod hand even faster and then stop it abruptly.

The stop is critical in delivering the full energy of the cast toward the target. Any immediate follow-through of the rod after the stop opens the loop and reduces line speed. Most casters make a short backcast stroke, stop the rod, and then drift back to get a longer casting stroke forward. Since the stop is so critical I believe it is more efficient to

go to where you end the backcast and then stop—eliminating the drift.

Instead of "power stroke" or similar terms, I use the term "speed-up-and-stop" to describe the period in which you accelerate the rod to a dead stop in the casting stroke. The speed-up-and-stop is one continuous motion, so I like to hyphenate the term when writing about it to convey that it is all one motion. The faster you accelerate the rod hand in the first portion of the casting stroke and the faster the hand speeds up and stops, the more energy the rod stores and the faster the line travels. Speed, not power, determines the efficiency of the cast.

You can deliver more powerful casts by using a longer stroke to increase line acceleration and the additional energy stored in the deeply bent rod. The farther back the rod bends, the more energy is stored in the rod for the moment you stop it. An easy way to demonstrate this is to have somebody hold the end of the fly line in his thumb and first finger while you bend

the tip of the rod; he can hold the line easily. Then if you walk away a few more feet and bend the rod more deeply, you can pull the line right out of his hand. The greater stroke length also gives you the option of making the cast almost immediately or anytime while your rod hand is moving forward. When you don't move the rod back far, timing the forward cast becomes more critical.

Principle 3

The line will go in the direction in which the rod tip speeds up and stops.

As the loaded rod sweeps forward, it bends under the strain of pulling on the line. During the speed-up-and-stop, the rod unbends or straightens, determining the direction of the cast. Also, as you speed up and stop, the rod tip does not travel in a straight path; it moves in a slight arc. The distance your rod tip descends from the beginning to the end of

Because the rod was extended well behind me and my rod hand traveled straight toward the target with rapid acceleration, the rod is deeply loaded. Two things that really make the cast go a long distance are how fast you accelerate the rod and how quickly you come to a stop.

For an elevated backcast, which prevents your line from hitting the water behind you, you must speed up and stop with the rod tip going up. With most forward casts, you should speed up and stop with the rod tip slightly rising. If the tip stops while going slightly downward, a larger loop occurs and sometimes causes the fly and line to crash to the surface.

the speed-up-and-stop determines the size of the loop. If you make a long speed-up-and-stop where the tip drops 3 feet from the start to the end of the stroke, you get a 3-foot loop. If your stroke is short and the tip only drops 4 inches, your loop will only be 4 inches.

Once the rod straightens on the stop, you cannot change the direction of the cast—you could throw the rod away and the line would still go in the direction of the stop. To be a little more specific, the line goes in the direction that the rod straightens when the rod hand stops. It is somewhat like shooting a gun. Once you pull the trigger and the bullet leaves the barrel, you could throw the gun away and the bullet would still travel to the target. Or once you throw a ball toward a target, its path cannot be changed. Anything that you do to the rod after you stop doesn't affect the direction of the

A fly rod is a flexible lever, and the farther back you bring it, the more it helps you make a cast. Notice how deeply this rod is bending.

With the rod extended well behind, the angler can pull out any imperfections and load the rod deeply. Starting with the rod well behind reduces the critical timing between a back and forward cast. My feet are spread wide apart to allow the rod arm to reach farther back and also allow the body to swivel more. This is not necessary for a short cast, but critical for longer casts.

loop. If you lower the rod, the line is lowered, but the fly still goes toward the target.

Understanding this important principle will help you monitor casting mistakes and adjust your stroke for different fishing situations. For instance, if you follow through even slightly after the speed-up-and-stop, the tip dips downward, you see sag in the line close to the rod, and some of the energy is directed downward and away from the target. Principle 1 tells us that sag is bad. To eliminate any sag on the backcast, always stop the rod tip while it is rising, in the direction you want the fly to travel.

Another situation where principle 3 comes into play is when attempting to make accurate casts with weighted flies such as beadhead nymphs, weighted Woolly Buggers, or bonefish patterns. Many right-handed casters tend to tilt the rod slightly to the right, so the weighted fly won't hit them on the forward cast. But on the stop the tip will flex slightly to the left, and since the line goes in the direction the tip stops, the weighted fly will curve to the left as it falls to the water. It is amazing how many people using weighted flies don't notice this. To get the most accurate forward cast, the rod tip should travel vertically and stop in the direction of the target.

Footwork is as important in fly casting as it is in other sports. When you are casting, your body should be able to move fluidly. When a right-handed person wants to throw a stone really far, he positions the right foot farther to the rear, and it is the same with a long fly cast. This allows the body to swivel until the chest is almost 90 degrees from the target and the arm to almost fully extend after the speed up and stop. Some anglers worry that pivoting the body will rock the boat in the shallows and send shock waves that alert the fish. If the body sways while pivoting, that's true. But if the body stays in a vertical position while pivoting to make a side cast, the boat doesn't rock.

Principle 4

The longer the distance the rod travels on the back and forward casting strokes, the less effort is required to make the cast.

A short back or forward rod stroke only bends the tip of the rod. As the rod moves through a longer stroke, the fly line continues to build line speed and increase the bend of the rod. What this means is that a caster with a shorter stroke must exert more effort to obtain the same line speed and load in the rod.

A fly rod is a flexible lever, and the farther back you bring it, the more it helps you make a cast. When making a short cast, you do not need to move the rod back far. When you have to cast farther, throw heavy or wind-resistant flies, defeat the wind, or make a number of special casts (even when trout fishing small streams), bring the rod farther back and forward.

The longer stroke also has the benefit of giving you more time to pull out any slack in the line. You can't make a forward cast until you move the line end. If there is a shock wave in the line, or if the wind pushes against the line, creating slack, that slack must be removed before a forward cast begins. The longer the rod travels forward, the more slack can be removed. If the rod stops near vertical, less slack can be removed and the cast becomes more difficult.

Picking Up Line

While it is not a casting rule, it is good fishing technique to lift all of the line from the surface before making a backcast. Ripping a fly line from the water can alert or frighten nearby fish and waste casting energy as the line is pulled free of surface tension. Quietly lift a floating line from the surface before the backcast, and roll-cast sinking lines to the surface before making a backcast. Practice will teach you how quickly to raise the rod.

To pick up line quietly, lower the rod tip to the surface and strip in the line to remove all slack. Slowly raise the rod to draw the line closer.

Concentrate on the end of the fly line as you raise the rod. If you raise the rod too slowly, the line will sag and the end will never come free of the surface. If you raise the rod too fast, you rip the line from the water, disturbing fish. When the line end leaves the surface but the leader is still in the water, make a backcast while the rod tip is rising to ensure there is no sag in the line.

A good backcast with little disturbance on the water.

Note how much disturbance there is on the water if you start picking up the fly line too early. As I lift the rod quickly while the fly line is on the water, surface tension grips the floating fly line.

Ripping the line loose from surface tension creates a huge disturbance that spooks fish.

CHAPTER 2

The Basic Overhead and Sidearm Casts

If you fish for different species or fish different waters, you have to adjust your tackle and technique. One day you may be casting near-weightless trout flies; the following week, air-resistant deer-hair bass bugs. On trout streams, short, accurate casts may be required one moment, but then the breeze kicks up, and you need to punch your casts into the wind to a fish feeding on the far side of the river. You may be on a guided trip, and one minute your guide rows you close to a pod of rising fish where distance isn't nearly as important as accuracy; on the way to the launch at dusk, he has you throwing large streamers with sinking lines against the bank for the river's large brown trout. If you learn to cast only one way, you limit both how you can fly-fish and what you can catch.

The traditional method of fly casting teaches anglers to use mainly the arm and the wrist to make all casts. Most of the casts are made in a vertical plane, where the rod tip moves back and forth between the often-quoted 10 o'clock and 2 o'clock positions. This works fine when casting light lines, rods, and flies at relatively short distances. But when throwing longer casts, especially with heavier rods, lines, and often weighted or air-resistant flies, this method is not only inefficient, it can cause serious physical problems, such as painful tennis elbow or torn rotator

cuffs. It also creates casting problems, such as tailing loops and the tangles that ensue. Since it requires strength, this method also prohibits older anglers and women who don't have powerful wrists and arms from expanding their horizons into saltwater or bass fishing, which require heavier tackle and longer casts.

Most fly fishers are taught the overhead cast first, and it is the most accurate short-range cast. The energy of the back and forward cast is directly away from and back to the target. A tilted or side cast with any weighted line or fly at the end of the cast tends to hook to one side or throw a curve in the final presentation.

Sidearm casts are useful whenever you are casting a heavy rod or a lot of line. When casting in the traditional overhead manner, most anglers can lift only so much line because of the limited range of motion, and to compensate they apply extra force during the speed-up-and-stop and the tip invariably dips downward. This creates sag that must be removed before a forward cast can start. With a sidearm cast, the rod continues to moves back and is able to lift con-siderably more line from the surface before the cast is made, and with a sidearm cast, the angler can stop while the rod is rising, which prevents sag.

Because the side cast allows you to position the rod well behind you,

you can make a longer forward stroke, which increases the load on the rod—storing extra energy for the forward cast. Bringing the rod back low also allows you to make some important fishing casts, such as the reach and stack casts.

The greatest advantage to a side cast is that it reduces the chances of getting a tennis elbow or torn rotator cuff, two painful problems that often occur when 8-weight or larger rods are used repeatedly to obtain distance and throw heavier lines and flies. During the vertical stroke, the angler flexes the wrist to help propel the line back and forth. Because of the short stroke in the overhead cast, the angler tries to compensate with power, generated at the expense of rotator cuffs stressed with each back and forth motion. Every time he flexes his wrist, there is a strain on the tendons attached at the elbow. In time, the rotator cuffs are often torn or tennis elbow develops.

Almost all serious fly fishermen who use heavier rods and lines and frequently cast long distances have complained about either a torn rotator cuff or tennis elbow or both. Neither of these painful experiences is necessary if the angler brings the rod sideways and well to the rear before starting the forward cast. If the cast is performed correctly, there is virtually no movement to the rotator cuffs or strain on the tendons attached to the elbow. Instead the cast is made with the body rather than just the wrist and arm. Learn this technique and you will reduce your chances of suffering from torn rotator cuffs or tennis elbow.

Keep in mind that absolute sidearm and absolute overhead are extremes. I often choose a casting position somewhere in between the two for midrange casts. For me, an angle between 45 and 60 degrees from vertical is the most comfortable and natural arm angle. My arm is angled enough that I can extend it, and my range of motion is not limited by taking the rod directly back and forward completely vertically. The longer the cast, the more your body should swivel and the farther you should pull your arm back.

The back and forward casts are subject to the basic principles of fly casting, but it may be necessary to make the backcast very different from the cast delivering the fly forward. Perhaps the most common example is where a

side backcast is needed, but a vertical forward cast is required. Such is the case when making a stack cast, casting shooting heads, casting weighted flies, and some other situations discussed in this book. Even when dry-fly fishing, you may want to combine the power and efficiency of a sidearm-style stroke with the accuracy of a vertical cast that comes straight over the rod tip.

In some of these sequences I am hauling—if you do not yet know how to haul, follow along anyway, and later, after spending some time with the chapter on hauling, you can come back. But the rod motions are the same regardless of whether you haul. Even when I am casting moderate distances, I often haul, and you probably will too once you read, study, and practice the techniques in chapter 4. I recommend that you, like I did, learn the basic casting motions first, get them down well, and then start introducing the haul into your repertoire.

The Grip

Gripping the fly rod is like gripping a baseball bat, golf club, or tennis racquet. If you are up at the plate and about to hit a ball, gripping the bat hard the entire time would compromise your swing, you wouldn't hit the ball very well, and your hands would hurt at the end of the day. Good hitters grip the bat just before they make contact with the ball. You don't grip your golf club hard the entire time you swing for a long drive; you squeeze it just before you hit the ball. When serving in tennis, you grip the racquet just as the ball makes contact with it, not through the entire swing. Instead, the club, bat, or racquet is held just firmly enough to control it through the stroke.

Through the fly-casting stroke, only grip the rod hard just before you speed up and stop. Blisters or red hands at the end of a practice session or day of fishing are signs that you are gripping the rod too hard.

The basic casting stroke is the same with fly, surf, plug, and spinning rods. The only difference is that you unroll the line toward the target with a fly rod. Note that I said "unroll" and not cast. In a basic fly cast (without shooting line) any line that is straight from the rod tip out is not moving, similar to tracks on a tank. The tracks on the bottom of the tank are stationary and the tracks on the front end are moving and pulling the tank along. The closer that the forward end of the line is to the stationary part of the line, the tighter the loop. When fly fishers think of casting the line, they tend to overpower the rod hand, which creates shock waves and other problems. Think of unrolling the line, and your presentations become smoother.

Overhead Cast

Begin the cast with the rod low and all slack removed.

Raise the rod to lift the line from the water, and as you do, keep your hand and elbow low. When the line is out of the water, make the backcast while the rod tip is still rising.

Speed up and stop to make the backcast, keeping the forearm and hand low. *I prefer not to flex the wrist.* The speed-up-and-stop is very short.

Keep your elbow on the shelf during the cast. During an overhead cast, this just means that you must not raise your elbow much higher than its normal resting position. Because the speed-up-and-stop was short, the rod tip stopped directly away from the target, and *because I did not flex my wrist,* the line is straight and the loop tight.

Begin the forward cast just before the line unrolls.

The low rod hand carries the rod straight forward toward the target. The speed-up-and-stop is brief with no flexing of the wrist so the tip stops parallel to the water.

A tight loop develops because I did not flex my wrist or flexed it only slightly during the short speed-up-and-stop.

Because my rod hand moved almost parallel to the surface during the back and forward cast and I flexed my wrist little or not at all, almost all the energy was directed away from and back to the target in the form of a small loop.

WATCH OUT FOR: Bent Wrist

As I lift line from the water, I start to raise my rod hand and begin the speed-up-and-stop with my rod hand high and wrist flexing back. The rod tip has traveled around a wide arc, creating a large loop.

As I sweep the rod forward, I begin to straighten my bent wrist. I bring the rod forward with my wrist cocked and rod hand high. During the speed-up-and-stop, my wrist bends forward to straighten and my rod hand begins dropping, forcing the rod tip to throw the line around a large curve, and a big loop develops. Note how far the rod sweeps downward.

WATCH OUT FOR: Twisting the Wrist

To compensate for the limited range of motion in the conventional overhead cast, some people twist their wrists outward so that they can take the rod farther back. As the rod lifts line from the water, my rod hand begins twisting outward. But this causes the line hand to unroll the line outward, and energy is wasted when not directed away from the target.

During the speed-up-and-stop for the backcast, I twist my wrist even more. This causes the line to unroll outward and not directly away from the target.

Twisting the wrist during the speed-up-and-stop on the forward cast will cause additional problems, such as the leader and fly jumping to the left as the cast ends.

Sidearm Cast

Begin the cast with the rod pointed at the fly and all slack removed. Tilt your rod at an angle, making sure that your thumb is opposite the target behind the grip. Begin to bring the rod back to your side. The rod hand should not be much higher than the elbow for best results. If the rod hand is held too high, there is a tendency for the rod to dip downward on the backcast.

As you take the rod back and up, begin hauling with your line hand. Watch the line and do not make the backcast until you lift all of it from the surface. Slide your elbow along the shelf and keep your thumb behind the handle as you lift the line from the surface. Your haul should mirror the length of the rod hand's acceleration.

As soon as the line end leaves the water, speed up and stop with your rod hand and haul simultaneously. The angle of the rod has been rising throughout the backcast. It is important that the rod tip not be higher than your head, though, so that the tip can stop while still rising, creating a flat, rising backcast.

With a sidearm cast, you can lift the line much farther back. Haul with your line hand during the entire period, and as soon as the line end leaves the water, speed up and stop with the tip rising on the stop. To make a long and efficient backcast, pivot your body and shift your weight to your back foot to aid the cast. If you need to make a longer forward casting stroke, let your arm drift farther back. It can rise slightly from the shelf at the very end of the stroke.

Just before the loop unrolls, begin the forward cast with the rod well behind your body.

Pivot your body back, aiding the cast as your elbow slides forward on the shelf while your arm accelerates forward and your line hand is hauling. Transfer your weight to the forward foot. Your elbow tracks along the shelf with your thumb behind the handle away from the target.

Before making the speed-up-and-stop, the rod has traveled a long distance. The longer the stroke, the more the rod can accelerate the line and the deeper it will bend. A brief speed-up-and-stop produces a tight loop, directing all the energy at the target.

Do not lower the rod until the line is unrolling.

Just before the line unrolls, lower the rod.

Sidearm Cast (Front View)

Begin with your right foot back, your elbow on the imaginary shelf, and the rod tip near the surface.

To make a good backcast, the line should travel directly away from the target. The rod tip should stop while it is rising to ensure a flat line on the backcast. To accomplish this, lay the rod over at 45 to 90 degrees from the body, so that you can lift a longer line from the water.

Keep your elbow on the shelf and thumb behind the rod handle away from the target. Do not flex your wrist on the backcast. Swivel your body, and if you move your elbow back along the shelf, your rotator cuff and the tendons at the elbow do not move. Hauling helps, especially on longer casts.

You are making most of the cast with your body, eliminating torn rotators and tennis elbow. If you need to make a much longer cast, put your right foot farther back and extend your forearm back farther. Allow the backcast to travel to the rear.

With a short cast, as shown here, you only need to swivel your body slightly as your forearm moves forward, with your elbow staying in contact with the shelf. Your body would have swiveled farther to the rear and back again for a longer cast.

If I raise my elbow off the shelf during the back or forward cast, I will open the loop. A tight loop results if your elbow tracks back and forth on the shelf. With a cast where your arm is fully extended on the back or forward cast, it is okay to raise your elbow slightly after the speed-up-and-stop. Lower the rod to a fishing position when the loop is well away from it.

Instinctive Casting

With most of the casting I teach, I find if you've never had a lesson, you do things naturally and instinctively. To make a good backcast, think about throwing a block to a person behind you. With this prop, I have often been able to teach someone how to make a natural backcast in minutes.

With your elbow in a natural resting position and thumb behind the small wood block, try to throw the block at a target slightly uphill behind you. This will teach you how to make the proper motion for a sidearm backcast.

For a short cast, sweep your hand back and uphill just a short distance. Release the block toward the target.

For a long backcast, shift your upper body more to the rear, while keeping your elbow on the imaginary shelf. Extend your arm well to the rear before releasing the block at an uphill angle toward the target. *Note that you did not naturally bend the wrist but kept it straight.* If the block does not go in the direction of the target, you stopped your hand in the wrong direction.

WATCH OUT FOR: Twisting the Wrist

I begin the cast with my thumb behind the rod handle away from the target.

As the speed-up-and-stop begins for the backcast, I have twisted my wrist.

This causes the rod tip to rotate around and outward.

The line is forced to travel out and around a wider loop.

The 45-Degree-Angle Cast

The 45-degree angle allows you to make effortless casts from 30 to 60 feet because you can move the rod and arm back farther. The cast starts with the rod tip low. Longer casts are easier if you pick up a good deal of line, which requires a low rod tip, no slack in the line, and often a haul.

Lift all line before backcasting.

Take the rod back, and angle and begin the backcast as soon as the line leaves the water. Haul during the length of the rod hand's acceleration. Your arm travels a short distance behind you before you accelerate to a stop with the tip rising, producing a tight loop.

The tight loop unrolls.

Just before the line unrolls, begin the forward cast.

Your elbow has remained on the imaginary shelf and your thumb behind your rod hand, away from the target.

Haul during the forward acceleration of the rod. Briefly speed up and stop above the target. Because of the brief speed-up-and-stop with the tip stopping straight ahead, a taut line with a small loop is delivering all the energy of the cast toward the target.

Front view of a 45-degree cast.

The loop is allowed to unroll well away from the rod tip.

Start to lower the rod. The line continues to straighten and fall to the water. The cast ends with a soft presentation.

Oval Cast

The backcast and the forward cast do not need to be in the same plane. One of the most effective casts for weighted flies, weighted lines, or leaders with split shot on them is what is commonly called an oval, or Belgian, cast. The horseshoe shape provides continuous tension on the rig and avoids an abrupt change of direction that often causes tangles.

Begin the cast with the rod low. As soon as the line end leaves the surface, make the backcast.

Bring the rod around for a vertical cast. Don't start the forward cast until the thumb is behind the rod hand, away from the target.

Allow the line to almost straighten.

Make the forward cast, keeping the thumb behind the rod hand, away from the target.

Speed up and stop the rod to form a nice loop.

Allow the loop to unroll away from the rod tip. When the loop is well away from the tip, you can start to lower the rod. Continue lowering the rod.

Cross-Shoulder Cast

By following the principles, you can adapt your cast to meet different fishing challenges such as wind or obstructions that interfere with the path of your rod tip. The cross-shoulder cast restricts the body's movements and is usually only effective at relatively short distances, but it is a good choice when the wind is blowing toward your casting arm side.

Keep Your Thumb Opposite the Target

Before you begin the backcast, position your thumb behind the rod handle, opposite the target. The most efficient cast is when the line unrolls directly away from (180 degrees) and then directly toward the target. (Some special casts require twisting the wrist, such as vertical curve casts, but they are exceptions.)

This is the correct thumb position for a vertical cast. Keeping your thumb behind the target on top of the cork grip is the grip that allows you to make the best stop with the rod. Keep your thumbnail traveling back away from and toward the target to keep the rod tip traveling straight. Many small-stream anglers put their pointer fingers on top of the cork, but that pointer finger is not nearly as strong as the thumb, so you can't accelerate or stop the rod as easily.

To make an angled cast, do not twist your wrist. Instead, move your forearm to keep the thumb behind the rod handle and away from the target.

To make a side cast, lower your forearm and still keep the thumb behind the rod handle away from the target. If you make a side backcast and a vertical forward cast, do not twist the wrist. Lay the forearm over with the thumb in the correct place and make a side cast. Move the forearm up to make a vertical forward cast.

CHAPTER 3

Casting with Control

If you can't shoot well, you can't hunt well. And if you cast poorly, you limit the number of fish you can catch. Some of the major destroyers of a good cast are not keeping your elbow on the shelf, twisting your wrist, and elevating the rod hand. Except for short casts, most problems tend to occur with a vertical backcast.

One of the biggest causes of tailing loops, wide loops, and shoulder injuries is not keeping your elbow on the shelf, which is an issue for most people when vertical casting. I reference the shelf a lot in the previous chapter, but it is

worth taking a closer look at it here because of its role in potentially giving you trouble with your loops. You should rarely elevate your elbow while casting. Imagine walking up to a shelf that is as high as your elbow. During most of the casting stroke, your elbow should remain on this imaginary shelf. If you watch many great casters using either one- or two-handed rods, they keep their elbows as if they are on that shelf and change the trajectory of their casts by the direction of the rod tip and hand stop. The elbow should track along the shelf for shorter casts. But

when you extend your rod hand well behind you, it is all right to raise your elbow slightly after the stop.

Raising the elbow off the shelf vertically or to the side tends to open the loop and reduces the total body movement. It forces you to use your arm and shoulder joint and less of your body to aid in long or more difficult casts. Longtime fly casters who develop rotator cuff problems almost always have been casting with their elbows raised high through the cast. With practice, you can become a good caster even if you raise your elbow on the backcast,

Making slight movements with your rod hand can move the rod tip quite a bit. If you grip the rod and bend your wrist back and forth, the rod butt only moves a few inches, but the tip is moving through a wide arc—perhaps 4 to 6 feet.

but this stresses or tears your rotator cuff, and since you tend to flex your wrist quite a bit, you could develop tennis elbow from casting heavier rods and flies. The higher above the imaginary shelf the elbow rises, the more the shoulder joint rotates. Keeping the elbow on the shelf and moving the body back and forth results in little or no rotation of the shoulder joint. All the energy of the cast is directed away from and back to the target, and little strength or effort is required.

On the backcast, I do not generally bend my wrist at all. I just make the whole cast with my forearm. When I come forward, I can carry my hand in a more level position, so I turn my forearm and wrist over until my thumb is parallel with the water at the end of the side or vertical cast. That tilts the rod down slightly, forms a tight loop, and prevents tailing loops. That is why, on the forward cast, I raise my elbow slightly as I duck the rod tip. Taking the elbow off the shelf to accomplish this move is okay.

Elbow on Shelf

Short Cast

Medium Cast

Long Cast

Because I moved my elbow from low to high, the rod is forced to throw the line around a curve.

Keep the elbow on the shelf as you direct the rod tip up and away from the target during the speed-up-and-stop, producing a nice loop.

Curing Tailing Loops

Tailing loops, when the leader or the front of the line tangles with the main line, plague casters who can cast beyond 45 feet. While tailing loops can occur anytime, they usually develop when you are casting vertically or with longer casts, especially when you make an extra effort to gain a greater distance than you can comfortably cast. You can tail the loop on the back or the forward cast, and some anglers are unaware that they frequently tail the backcast. The resulting knots in the leader are often referred to as wind knots, but they are really bad casting knots. The angler would get them on a calm day as well as on a windy one.

Remember casting principle 3—the line goes in the direction the rod tip speeds up and stops. Almost all tailing loops occur when the rod tip speeds up and stops in a straight path, and the line collides with itself. Straight path does not necessarily mean parallel to the water. It can be at any casting angle—the rod tip can stop going up, parallel to the water, or down toward the surface. The most common cause of a tailing loop is elevating the elbow on the backcast and lowering it on the forward cast. You can also get a tailing loop if the backcast drops so low that it travels below the rod tip throughout the forward cast. Almost no one makes such a bad backcast, so for practical purposes, we can eliminate this reason. Some anglers will accelerate forward with the rod, pause, and then begin accelerating again, causing a tailing loop. Fortunately, both of these mistakes rarely occur.

Some common explanations for tailing loops range from shocking the rod during the forward cast, to beginning the forward cast too soon or too late, to moving the rod tip in a concave manner. If you shock the rod with the tip stopping straight ahead, you will get a tailing loop. Beginning the forward cast too soon, overpowering the cast, and starting the speed-up-and-stop too late in the cast all have a tendency to cause the rod tip to speed up and stop in a straight path. If the rod tip travels in a concave manner, you'll get a tailing loop, but this is because you drove the rod handle straight forward. By keeping the elbow on the shelf throughout the cast you almost automatically eliminate tailing loops.

As long as the top of the loop remains on the top, and the bottom on the bottom, there will be no tailing loop. When you make a cast in either direction, the bottom of a loop is at the tip of the rod. To eliminate almost all the tailing loops, the rod tip must get out of the way of the incoming line to avoid running into itself. To eliminate most tailing loops, you need only to do two things: Keep your rod hand at the same height or level throughout the forward cast and stop the rod with your forearm and thumb parallel to the water's surface. This may widen the loop, but you will prevent tailing loops.

Avoiding Tailing Loops

Start with the rod tip low to the water. The lower your rod hand at the beginning of the forward cast, the less likely it is that a tailing loop will occur. Lift the rod to draw the line toward you. The ideal height for most casts is when your rod hand at the end of the backcast is just above the height of your elbow. Just before the backcast unrolls, begin the forward cast. Note the height of the rod as the forward cast starts.

Accelerate the rod forward. Your elbow remains on the shelf and your thumb is behind the rod handle away from the target.

Your rod hand stays at the same height throughout the forward cast. Speed up and stop with your forearm and thumb parallel to the surface so the rod tip ducks away from the oncoming line, eliminating the possibility of a tailing loop.

If your thumb points upward on the speed-up-and-stop, the tip will stop in a straight path and a tailing loop will occur (because the rod tip was forced to travel in a straight path). If your thumb points downward on the stop, there will be no tailing loop, but the loop will be larger.

Demonstrating Tailing Loop

To teach people how to cast, you need to learn to re-create common casting errors like tailing loops. In this sequence, we will purposely cast a tailing loop. I begin the cast with the rod tip low to the water.

As I lift the line for the backcast, my elbow rises off the shelf and my rod hand is above my head.

As the line unrolls, and the backcast nears the end, my rod hand and elbow are elevated.

As I begin the forward cast I lower my hand and elbow. As soon as the rod bends on the forward cast, the line is aimed directly at the rod tip.

As my rod hand continues to drop, it causes the rod tip to speed up and stop in a straight path. The tip does not duck under the oncoming line, and the line behind runs into the line in front of it, creating a tailing loop. The tailing loop will either tangle or create a knot in the line or leader.

Controlling Loop Size

The most efficient cast has high speed and a small loop that unrolls directly away from and then directly toward the target. Large vertical or side loops distribute the cast's energy around a curve and not to the target and are more air-resistant than small ones. Another way to say this is that the larger the loop you unroll, either to the side or vertically, the more atmosphere the line goes through. Something has to hold a large loop open, and that steals energy from the cast.

Once the rod is bent, straining against the line, on either the backcast or forward cast, the line is taut and aimed at the rod tip. In casting, the rod hand is a pivot causing the tip of the rod to travel in an arc. During the speed-up-and-stop, the tip will duck away from the oncoming line. The farther the tip dips away from the line, the larger the loop. The shorter the speed-up-and-stop, the less the rod tip dips and the tighter the loop.

The most efficient cast is when the line unrolls directly away from and then unrolls directly toward the target. A large line loop (vertical or horizontal) dissipates energy away from the target. Most of the time, twisting the wrist will cause the line to unroll outward, wasting energy. Unless carefully controlled, flexing the wrist during the casting stroke enlarges the loop—wasting energy. The less the wrist is flexed when fishing heavier tackle or making longer casts, the less likely it is that the angler will develop tennis elbow.

Many people don't cast tight enough loops, and they also don't understand that it is important to know how to make different size loops to adjust to various fishing situations. To quickly teach people to cast tight loops, I ask them to look at the tip while false-casting and imagine they are throwing the line at the rod tip during the back and forward cast. This works for beginners as well as more advanced casters.

It is important that the angler have a background that allows him or her to clearly see the rod tip and line. A vertical cast viewed against a bright sky is often difficult to see. A side or angled cast is usually best. I ask the student to strip off about 12 feet of line plus the leader, and I ask him to relax as I hold his hand and make the first several false casts, emphasizing that the purpose is to make the line strike the rod tip. Once he understands this, I remove my hand. Usually he immediately begins throwing a tight loop.

Too often when I am teaching, the caster makes a few tight loops and starts to admire them rather than continuing to look at the tip. Inevitably, the loops get bigger because the caster is not focusing on the rod tip with the line.

In almost every sport, we have been taught to follow through, but if you want tight loops, don't follow through after the stop. The bottom of a loop is at the tip of the rod and follow-through simply drags the loop open. This is a common fault with many anglers on their final cast. They will false-cast tight loops with no follow-through, and on the last cast as soon as they speed up and stop, they follow through, tearing the loop open. The speed-up-and-stop and the haul should cease at the same moment. Perhaps the most common fault of double haulers is that on the forward cast they continue to haul after the rod stops. Of course, this pulls the tip downward, opening the loop and reducing distance.

Perfecting Practice

No matter how much you practice, it won't help unless it is good practice. Practicing poor techniques means that you will later have to unlearn your mistakes. Also, don't practice for too long, or you will get tired and your practice will be ineffective. Practice sessions should not be longer than 15 minutes. Two 15-minute sessions are usually much better than an hour-long session. Roll and Spey casts and picking up a lot of line for distance casting can't be practiced in a parking lot, so when possible, try to practice on water. But don't practice while you are fishing; focus only on practicing. You also need to be able to see the fly line, so use a bright-colored one and wear a cap that doesn't obstruct your view of the entire fly cast, as some long-brim hats do. Also, wear sunglasses to protect your eyes from stray casts. Practice should also be fun.

Lawn Practice

In this exercise, the angler teaches himself how to cast tighter loops. The equipment is simple, inexpensive, and easily available. Two 50-foot, 1/4-inch-thick nylon clothesline ropes work fine, or a pair of 50-foot garden hoses also will do. When I use ropes, I attach long nails to the rope ends, which I then push into the ground to ensure the ropes stay taut during the exercise. In the photos, we are using two fly lines still attached to reels, which also work well.

To teach someone how to cast tighter loops, I set the parallel ropes about 6 feet apart—resembling a pair of railroad tracks. The caster should stand so that the rod tip is about a foot inside the nearest rope and ready for a backcast. All casts are made close to the ground. During each cast, he should attempt to keep the fly line and the rod tip inside the ropes. If, at the end of each cast, the rod tip or any portion of the fly line is outside the two ropes, the loop is too large. Every time a backcast or forward cast ends, the caster should stop and examine the effort. One soon sees that the more you bend the wrist, the larger the line loop.

When he is able to make a series of casts with the line and rod inside the two ropes, I narrow the gap between the two ropes to 4 feet. When he is successful at this, I have him false-cast using sidestrokes, trying to keep the line in the air between the two ropes. Gradually I have him elevate to a vertical position and learn how to throw tight loops from side, angled, and vertical positions. For most students, in 20 minutes they are throwing great loops, and best of all, they are teaching themselves. The caster masters tight loops when he can cast the fly line between two ropes that are only about 30 inches apart. Be sure to stop after every back and forward cast and evaluate the results. Don't rush through this exercise.

Stand far enough back so that the rod tip is just inside the near line at the start of the backcast. Your elbow should be on the imaginary shelf and your thumb behind your rod hand from the center of the parallel lines in front. All casts are made low to the grass, not elevated.

Keep the rod and line low to the grass during each cast. After the backcast, stop and examine the line. If the line and rod tip are inside the parallel lines, a tight loop has formed. Stop after each cast to monitor what you are doing right and wrong.

Repeat on the forward cast. This line travels in the center of the two parallel lines because a proper tight loop was made. This is the result you are working for. By stopping after each cast to examine the line, you are able to make adjustments and soon throw tight loops.

If you twist your wrist during any cast, it tends to open loops, and energy is directed away from the target. You'll soon see that twisting your wrist during a cast detracts from its effectiveness.

This is not what you want to do. Both the rod tip and the line are outside the parallel lines because a large loop was created.

Once you have learned to make tight loops and keep the rod tip and line inside the parallel ropes, you are ready for the next step. Instead of stopping after each cast, begin false-casting above the parallel lines, concentrating on keeping the rod tip and line inside on the backcast.

Hula Hoop

Even if an angler can cast tight loops, many can't do so accurately, and the hula hoop is an excellent tool to improve that. Hula hoops come in many sizes, but the standard 32-inch hoop available in many department stores is best to start with.

You can secure a hula hoop to a pole with tape, but often the leader or line snags or tangles between the pole and hoop. I like to have an "arm" extending from the support pole past the top of the hula hoop. The bottom of the hoop should be positioned about 3 feet above the ground. Without a fly or tuft of yarn on your leader, begin about 30 feet from the hoop and attempt to cast the line (not just the leader) through the hoop. When you are able to get eight out of ten casts through the hoop, back away to 40 feet and repeat. When you can throw at least five out of ten casts through the hoop at 50 feet, you have really mastered loop control. Fly-fishing clubs and groups can have fun by holding informal contests to see how successful members are at throwing a number of casts through the hoop. When you can consistently cast loops through the hoop at a range of distance from 30 to 60 feet, try casting with your other hand or try casting through the hoop on your backcast.

Stand about 25 feet from the hoop for the first practice session. Use a brightly colored hoop and a bright fly line. Note that the rod tip remains where the speed-up-and-stop occurs. This ensures a tight loop. Fly fishermen quickly learn, when trying to throw through the hoop, that following through after the speed-up-and-stop creates a loop too large to enter the hoop.

As the loop nears the target, you can lower the rod.

Force

Good fly casters are constantly monitoring and regulating their line speeds as they adjust to different conditions. Sometimes you need to accelerate rapidly in the casting stroke: If you want to make a tuck or curve cast, the faster you speed up and stop, the greater the curve you are going to get in the line or the more the line tucks under the rod tip in a tuck cast. At other times, like when making a stack cast or another dry-fly presentation, you want a relatively gentle forward cast. Knowing when to apply force and when to cast softly allows you to cast more efficiently throughout the day.

Tight, fast loops are not always the best result. They are the most efficient, but there are many times when making presentations to fish that you don't want a fast, tight loop. When dry-fly fishing, for instance, I often deliberately open

my loop not only to prevent tailing loops, but also to slow down and soften the presentation of the cast. Most slack-line casts are better made with a gentle forward cast. If you make the forward cast part of a stack cast with great force, the line will sail out, get to the end, kick, and recoil back, and you'll have a terrible, uncontrolled cast. The same thing applies on a reach cast. In a good reach cast, the line travels high above the water, but very slowly, and that gives you the opportunity to lay the line to one side. If the line is traveling fast, particularly low and fast, you don't have the time to make a good reach. Another time where you would not use a high-speed line is when you want to make an aerial mend. With an aerial mend, you stop the rod high, with only enough speed to get the fly to the target. And then you decide where you want to make the mend. If

you generate high line speed, you won't give the mend the time it needs to form and fall to the water.

You also don't want to use force when you are casting weighted shooting heads and sinking lines. You do move the line fast through the backcast, but the forward cast should be gentle. As we discuss in the chapter on casting weighted flies, if you come forward with too much force, the end of the sinking line tends to dump on you. It's almost like when a dog runs out of leash and the force knocks him back. If you are throwing with the wind, you need to make a tight backcast, but on your forward cast you should not apply that much force because the wind is going to carry your line. When you cast into the wind, you do the opposite, driving your forward cast toward the water with high line speed.

Trajectory

An important and often ignored aspect of presentation is the angle at which you direct the fly line on the forward cast. Many people cast at the same angle all the time, but good casters modify the trajectory of the cast depending on fishing conditions. With weighted flies, for instance, I make most of my forward casts directing the fly above eye level so that it is slightly climbing. Weighted flies splash too much if the cast is directed toward the water and can spook fish. Also, the upward trajectory ensures that heavier flies will reach their target (this applies to weighted lines as well). When casting in the wind, the angle at which you aim your line can make or break the cast—you should drive the line to the water when casting into a wind, but when the wind is at your back, stop the rod tip while it is climbing.

Angle for casting into the wind.

Angle for casting weighted flies.

Casting in Wind

When casting into the wind, if you elevate the cast once the leader unrolls, the fly will be blown short of the target. Instead, speed up and stop so the fly is directed at the surface area of the target so when the leader unrolls the fly is in the water and cannot blow back.

Use this same technique when there is a strong side wind. If the wind blows from your casting arm side you need to make a side cast that will keep the fly away from you, and then make a vertical forward cast directing the fly at the target surface area. Once the rod stops giving direction to the fly, lower the rod tip into the water, which places all the fly line on the water so it can't be blown to the side.

When making a stack cast, or if the wind is behind you and you want to shoot for distance, aim your cast high.

Accuracy

Whether casting to rising trout or hitting the holes in the lily pads when fishing popping bugs for largemouth bass, the more accurate you are, the more fish you will catch. Everything from large tarpon to small brook trout demands accuracy.

To be accurate, you must first have a specific target. Consider a hunter who shoots a deer. The hunter does not shoot *at* the deer. He would probably miss it. Instead he aims at a very specific area of the deer's body. So it is with accurate fly casting to small and hard-to-hit targets. You should not cast to the shoreline; instead focus on a very small target.

When casting to a fish, you often do not want the fly to hit the fish. Your target might be 2 feet upstream of a feeding trout or 10 feet in front of a cruising bonefish. Instead of casting at the fish, you should concentrate on where you want to the fly to land, while watching the fish in your peripheral vision.

You can get extreme accuracy with a fly rod if you cast the line in a slightly climbing manner with enough energy to go beyond the target. Instead of releasing the line, shoot it through an O formed with your first finger and thumb (acting like a rod guide as line flows through it), and as the fly nears the target, compress the two fingers to slow the line's flight speed. When the fly is over the target, trap the line so the fly falls where you want it. If the line flows through your two fingers, it is also under your control at all times. If you suddenly realize the cast is going wrong, trap the line and make another backcast and forward cast. If you release the line during its flight, you have to look down to recover it after the fly lands. That means taking your eyes off the fish and risking not being able to locate it again.

Mousetrap Practice

Few fly fishermen realize that on almost every cast made with a weighted fly, they throw an inaccurate curve in the leader and fly. If you are a right-handed caster, chances are you tilt the fly rod tip outward as you make the forward cast, and since the line goes in the direction the rod tip speeds up and stops, when the rod tip flexes to the left, the leader and fly swing to the left. Of course, if you are a left-hander, the fly will curve to the right. This is the main reason why freshwater trout fishermen throw an inaccurate cast with weighted flies—especially nymphs. To make an accurate cast, you can make any kind of backcast (side, angled, or vertical), but at the finish of the forward cast, the rod must be in a vertical position so the tip can stop in line with the target.

If you want to learn how to throw your fly with pinpoint accuracy, the mousetrap (or rat trap) is the tool for you. Not only is it effective, but it is a lot of fun to practice with. I like to print fish names on the trap treadle, such as tarpon, brown trout, etc. Cock the trap and set it about 20 feet from the caster so that it is easily visible. Use a weighted fly with the bend and point cut off. Ideal flies are weighted Woolly Buggers, small Clouser Minnows, or bonefish flies. Use a leader about 8 or 9 feet long. Locate the mousetrap about 20 feet away and use a leader of about 9 or 10 feet with a weighted fly. Remove the bend and point of the fly with wire cutters. If the weighted fly strikes the treadle, the trap snaps shut and leaps into the air.

Even the very best casters rarely hit the trap more than once or twice in twenty casts, but good casters will get close to the trap nearly every cast. Dragging the fly over the trap to spring it doesn't count—you have to hit it with the cast. Your first few casts may

The first few casts may be way off target, but as you continue casting the flies, your accuracy should improve. This is because you are now concentrating on the small target. Regardless of the angle of the backcast, if you bring the rod forward in a vertical plane and directed at the mousetrap, the line and fly will travel straight toward the trap.

be all over the place, but as you begin to concentrate on the tiny trap, your accuracy greatly improves. I have used the mousetrap for years in casting clinics. It is amazing how many good trout fishermen have played with the mousetrap and suddenly realized they have been throwing an inaccurate curve cast with their weighted nymphs and streamers.

CHAPTER 4

Mastering the Double Haul

The single and double haul are two of the most important techniques you can master. The single haul is nothing more than a pull with the line hand while the rod hand is making the cast. When you make two single hauls, one corresponding to the front cast and the other to the backcast, you are double-hauling. Double hauls help you load the rod and generate higher line speeds and are useful for everything from delivering a dry fly a short distance to propelling a huge streamer to a billfish.

There are two parts to any casting stroke: an acceleration (short or long) of the rod and then a stop. The acceleration of the rod accomplishes two things: It causes the line to increase its speed either away from or toward the target and bends the rod, storing energy. Following this motion is the speed-up-and-stop that causes the line to unroll to the target. Most anglers use the haul for the first part of a cast, the acceleration. Hauling the line makes it go faster and deepens the bend in the rod, storing additional energy, which results in a longer cast. But to improve the efficiency of the haul, the line hand should mirror the rod hand during a cast.

To understand how to improve the double haul, try this experiment: Make several false casts using the double haul, and on the final forward cast, accelerate the rod and release the line after the acceleration but *without* mak-

ing the speed-up-and-stop! Hauling increased the line speed and deepened the bend in the rod, but when you released the line, it traveled only a short distance. Repeat the experiment, but this time add a speed-up-and-stop to the forward cast, and the line sizzles toward the target. Without a stop, most of the energy is wasted.

The length of a double haul is dictated by fishing conditions and what you want to accomplish. When you are casting a dry fly, the haul may only be a few inches. If you're trying to throw a heavy line and weighted fly into a stiff breeze, the haul may be extra long. One of the keys to efficient hauling is to pull on the line during the rod's acceleration. If the rod is accelerated a short distance, so is the haul. If a longer acceleration occurs, the haul mirrors the length of the acceleration. Many use only a short, fast haul at the end of the stroke. By hauling during all of the rod's acceleration, you gain more line speed and load the rod more deeply.

To improve hauling efficiency, the moment the haul is completed on the backcast, raise your line hand toward the rod butt to reduce any slack. Body movement helps when making longer casts or when extra effort is required while hauling. If you stand squarely facing the target, you can only move the rod back so far. But if you drop your right foot back to the rear (if you are a right-handed caster) and swivel

your upper body so your chest is at a right angle to the target (you can still look at the target), you can bring your casting arm and rod farther to the rear. Remember principle 4: The longer the rod moves through the stroke, the more it aids the effort, and the longer the rod is swept forward, the longer the haul can be. This further increases line speed and loads the rod.

When you need more out of a cast, never get it with the rod hand; instead change the hauling speed. Most people haul at the same speed for every cast, but a single or double haul is like a gearshift, and the speed of the haul should change for different fishing conditions. Try this experiment to improve your double haul: Make a series of false casts but with every other cast, move your line hand faster. You will immediately note that as the line hand increases speed on the haul, the line travels faster. To learn how to haul faster without casting too hard with the rod hand (a common tendency), try holding the rod with only your thumb and first two fingers (for ladies who may not be as strong as men, I recommend holding the rod with the thumb and three fingers). It is impossible to overpower the rod holding it this way, and you will quickly learn to increase hauling speed without overpowering the rod hand.

During the haul, the action of your line hand should mirror your speed-up-and-stop casting stroke to produce more line speed and distance. The shorter and faster the rod tip moves during that speed-up-and-stop, the farther the line will unroll. To make the most effective double haul, you must mirror the motion of the rod. Most fishermen haul on the line continuously throughout the backcast and again throughout the forward cast, which is applying the same effect to the cast as if the rod sweeps backward and forward like a windshield wiper, without employing the speed-up-and-stop of the rod tip. Like the rod stroke, the most efficient haul should have two parts: a relatively long pulling on the line (to mirror the cast's first part) and a short, fast speed-up-and-stop (to mirror the cast's second part). When the rod speeds up and stops, the hauling hand should greatly accelerate in a short, fast speed-up-and-stop motion that mirrors the rod tip's action. The rod tip's speed-up-and-stop and the haul's short, fast speed-up-and-stop should be simultaneous. The long pull on the line (a windshield-wiper stroke) helps bend or load the rod. If the speed-up-and-stop of the tip and the greatly accelerated second phase of the haul start and stop at the same time, line speed will dramatically increase and you'll shoot more line.

Learning to double-haul is difficult because there is so much to do in such a short time. I teach my students to haul on the grass first because at the end of each cast they can examine and evaluate the forward and backcasts individually. With this method, I have taught many people how to double-haul in a few minutes. Of course, they will have to practice to perfect it. The slower someone performs the early motions, the faster they learn them. The faster you try to learn the technique, the longer it takes to learn. Do this exceptionally slowly and allow the line to fall to the grass after each back and forward cast. Then do not make another cast until you've determined how poorly or well you made that particular cast.

Hauling on the Grass

Start with about 20 feet of fly line plus the leader outside the rod tip. The cast will be made sideways and close to the grass. Do not throw an elevated cast.

Your line hand is close to the reel. Your elbow will stay on the imaginary shelf, and your thumb begins the cast behind the reel handle. Your wrist should not twist throughout the cast. Slowly slide the rod tip back just above the grass. Your line hand follows the reel.

Make a speed-up-and-stop to throw the backcast inches above the grass. At the same time you are accelerating on the backcast, pull quickly only a few inches with your line hand. This is a single haul.

As the backcast unrolls behind, rotate your body and position the rod opposite the target well behind you. Later you will learn to make longer hauls on the line, but for a beginner, the short haul makes for faster learning. It is important to turn your body. Later, when you want to cast longer, by turning your body you allow the rod to travel farther back, making a longer and more efficient stroke on the forward cast. You are also able to examine what you did right or wrong on the hauling backcast.

Before the backcast ends, move your line hand back in front of the reel. The cast will end. Allow the line to lie on the grass and examine how well you made the cast. The line hand should return close to the reel after each haul. If you spread the two hands apart as the rod makes another cast, the hands move toward each other, creating slack that must be removed before casting can begin. Returning the line hand close to the reel each time before starting the next cast eliminates slack, which not only makes your cast inefficient but can also result in the line tangling in the reel.

Slowly begin moving your rod hand forward, with your line hand moving forward close to the reel. And if you are confused, stop—think about what to do and then continue slowly forward. Continue to slowly move the rod forward just above the grass. Concentrate on the fact that you are going to make a forward cast and haul at the same time. Almost everyone has more trouble perfecting the forward haul than the back one, so don't be discouraged if at first things go poorly. The slower you do the exercise, the more time you have to consider and practice how to do it correctly.

Simultaneously accelerate the rod and pull on the line (hauling) a short distance to make the forward cast.

As you finish the cast, allow the line to fall to the ground and make sure your line hand has returned to its position in front of the reel. Again think about what you have done right and wrong. Once you have the technique going well, make the back and forward casts faster—and then elevate the rod and try hauling with a side cast so you can watch the line. Eventually you'll make a mistake. Place the line on the grass and repeat the early practice session. Usually, after several such practice sessions, you will be hauling well.

Hauling on the Water

Lower the rod tip to the surface and remove any slack. Lift the rod to move the line toward you and off the water. The line hand should follow the reel. If not, as the cast ends, the two hands are apart, creating possible slack that must be removed before the forward cast begins. When you practice this on the water, the water helps deepen the load in the rod.

Your line hand should follow the rod as it is lifted. Watch the end of the line.

The moment the line end leaves the water, the rod and line hand should begin accelerating.

If you need a longer cast or more speed, the rod and line hand accelerate simultaneously over a longer stroke. This is a relatively long cast, and the haul is long. For a shorter cast, you would only need a short haul.

It is vital that your rod hand's speed-up-and-stop and the hauling stop at the same time. It is the abruptness of the stop that is so important in projecting the line away from or toward the target. A common mistake is to continue to haul after the backcast speed-up-and-stop, which causes the rod to continue to flex, wasting energy.

The moment the hauling motion stops, move your hand toward the rod butt. Do not leave your hauling hand well away from the rod. This creates slack as the rod hand moves forward that must be removed before the forward cast begins. It also may cause the line to tangle around the rod butt or reel.

Just before the backcast unrolls, your line hand should be positioned near the rod butt. Just before the line unrolls, the rod and line hand begin accelerating forward.

Continue to accelerate both hands.

Both hands simultaneously stop at the end of the forward cast.

If you want to control the cast, shoot the line through your hand. When the line has almost completely unrolled toward the target, lower the rod while still controlling the shooting line. Just before the fly touches down, the rod line moves near the rod. When all line has been shot through the guides, you can place the line in your rod hand to begin a retrieve.

All line has been shot through the guides and you can place the line in your rod hand to begin a retrieve.

WATCH OUT FOR: Hauling After Rod Hand Stops

The more abruptly the rod stops, the more energy is directed at the target. The rod and line hand should mirror one another and work in unison. When both hands stop at the same time, all energy is directed at the target. In this example, the forward cast begins with both hands accelerating simultaneously.

The speed-up-and-stop occurs, but my line hand continues hauling, and the rod tip doesn't stop.

Even as the rod is lowering, I am still hauling on the line, detracting from the forward cast. Try this experiment: Make a fairly long backcast, and allow the line to lie straight on the ground behind you. Make a forward cast and continue pulling on the line after the rod hand speeds up and stops, and then release the line. Repeat this several times. Then make the same cast several times, with the line lying on the ground behind you, and make sure that both hands stop at the same time. Your loop will be tighter, and you'll cast farther.

Another common problem when hauling is to pull downward on the line during the backcast and leave your line hand well away from the rod. As the rod is swept forward, whether your line hand is stationary or brought upward, slack is increased between your line hand and your rod hand. You must remove this slack before the rod can pull on the line. The line hand makes a long pull. Because of the long hauling motion and leaving the hand so low, the line tends to fall beneath the rod butt as the backcast nears an end.

If my line hand remains in this position on the forward cast, the butt of the rod or the reel will trap the line underneath it.

As I lower the rod, the line will be tangled in either the reel or the rod butt. No retrieve is possible until the line can be untangled. This could be avoided if I had moved my line hand close to the rod butt as soon as the hauling motion had ceased.

Hauling Exercises

In addition to casting on the grass (see page 47), you can also do a few other exercises to improve the speed and timing of your haul: Try casting with two fingers or with just half a rod. Even if you think you are double-hauling efficiently, try these exercises to evaluate your haul.

When a fly fisherman needs to make a cast outside his range, the routine usually goes like this: While double-hauling, he makes two nice false casts, and then on the final forward cast—as if to give the cast a boost with some extra strength—he powers forward on the cast, often shocking the rod or opening the loop so much that the cast falls far shorter than it would have if he just released the line with no extra effort. Instead of trying to add extra force or power to the rod hand, work on your line hand technique to cast farther.

Most fly fishermen haul at about the same speed all the time. Instead, think of the haul like a gearshift. You should increase the speed of your haul when you need extra distance or speed, such as when casting into the wind, throwing heavier flies, or making longer casts. This makes the line travel faster and deepens the bend in the rod. But if you apply extra force with the rod hand, the forward cast almost always suffers.

When learning to haul extra fast, anglers tend to use extra force with the rod hand, creating shock waves and spoiling the cast. When teaching anglers to haul faster, I ask them to hold the rod with the thumb and first two fingers when false-casting. Now it is difficult to use too much power on the cast while hauling extra fast. Soon they realize the extra speed and distance come from the line hand, and they avoid overpowering the rod hand.

Two Fingers Exercise

Grip the rod with your thumb and two fingers and make your backcast by hauling faster than you would normally. After the backcast, begin with a much faster haul on the forward cast. Note that three fingers are holding the rod while the line hand is accelerating much faster than normal. Because it is impossible to overpower your rod hand with your thumb and two fingers, the loops are fine—teaching that not overpowering is the key when hauling faster to obtain greater distance.

Half a Rod Exercise

A rod is a flexible lever, and the longer the rod, the more it helps the cast. Casting with half a rod will quickly show you the limitations of your current hauling technique and force you to improve it. Once you cast better with half a rod, your casting really improves with the whole one. Practice without a fly since the line will often travel close to you. String the line through the forward half of the rod. Because you don't have a handle to hold, you must grip the lower half of the rod tip with your first finger lying along the rod as shown in the photo.

Extend about 20 feet of line outside the rod tip and begin false-casting. At first it may not go well because you are trying to cast with your rod hand. Back off on using force with your rod hand and increase the hauling speed, and suddenly the line and rod come alive. With practice, you can cast up to 70 feet with only a half rod.

CHAPTER 5

Going for Distance

n most freshwater situations, anglers who can cast 45 or 50 feet can handle just about any casting chore that confronts them. Trout fishermen generally cast no more than 50 feet. Things are different when you go for steelhead in salt water or Atlantic salmon on big rivers. The ability to throw a longer line becomes vital to success. This is not to say that you shouldn't try to get close to fish if possible, but many times that just isn't possible.

There are a hundred situations where having an extra 20 or 30 feet in your cast can make all the difference in the world. Sometimes you can't move closer to the fish, whether you are limited because of water depth or other conditions, or you don't have enough time to get closer. In many freshwater situations, the angler can move around, get into position, and then cast. In salt water you frequently have to make a quick cast from where you are, and it may not be the best position. Or the wind may be blowing so hard that you need to cast 80 feet to get 35. Unfortunately, nature doesn't let saltwater fly fishermen cast downwind very often. Salt water, lakes, and big rivers have few wind-free days. Another common situation where you need to make a longer cast is when you are blind-fishing. A long retrieve is often many times more productive than a short one. When you are working open water, the longer you can swim the fly, the more likely you are to put it in front of a fish. Many anglers (who generally can't cast very far) counter that you can't hook fish at long distances. This is true for giant tarpon and billfish that have hard mouths, but almost all other species can be hooked at great distances if you hold the rod low during the retrieve and the hooks are sharp. If you cannot consistently cast beyond 50 feet, I urge you to try to improve your distance. It's true that you can catch a lot of fish closer than 50 feet, but it is no shame to be able to effortlessly throw a long line.

One of the keys to distance casting is a good backcast. The rod tip must stop while it is rising to make a flat backcast with a tight loop.

Elements of Distance Casting

Anyone with skill can throw up to 80 or 90 feet with most lines. Beyond that distance, you need strength to sweep a rod through a long stroke at an ever-increasing speed and then bring it to an abrupt stop. Only strong people can accelerate the rod incredibly fast and then stop the tip dead to deliver all the energy toward the target. Many young or strong anglers can throw incredibly long distances (but in my view inefficiently) because they have the strength for the incredibly rapid stroke and are able to stop the rod abruptly. Were they efficient casters, they could increase their distance even more.

Tackle

Modern fly rods are moderate or fast action. I haven't seen what I regard as a slow-action rod in the past decade. A moderate-action rod will bend farther down from the tip than a fast-action rod under equal tension. For good casters, a fast-action rod can store more energy and stop quicker—simply because it is a bit stiffer. However, for most fly fishermen, stiffer rods require a greater sense of timing when casting. Rods rated for lines from size 1 to 6 are generally designed for presentation and will be slower, allowing the fly to be presented to the fish quietly, and they are almost always used by freshwater trout fishermen. Rods rated for 8- to 10-weight lines are designed for transportation and will cast a fly a long distance. Often, delicate presentations are not a consideration. Rods rated for 12-weight and higher may cast moderately well at relatively short distances but are designed for fighting giant tarpon and offshore species that, once brought to boatside, must be lifted to be caught or to be released. The 7- to 11-weight rods are like the 16-gauge shotgun—a little too much for some situations, and not enough for others, although there are some situations where they are just right.

The size of the stripping guide on the butt section can affect casting distance. When you shoot line, the line is traveling at a high speed, undulating, and does not slide through the guide easily. If you use a larger guide (just as we do with spinning rods), the line is less constricted and flows more easily through to the target. Manufacturers have to sell you what you want to buy, and many anglers will not purchase a rod with an extra-large butt guide. I would suggest that all rods 8 through 10 have a butt guide no less than 20 mm, and a slightly larger guide is even better. If you don't know how to replace your smaller guide, any competent fly shop can do this for you.

Fly lines can also influence how far you can cast. Lines designed with longer heads are best. Some will measure more than 65 feet from the front to the end of the back taper. Manufacturers sometimes indicate that such lines are for distance casting. After the angler false-casts and releases the line toward the target, the thick portion of the head exiting the rod tip easily supports the bottom of the loop and a smooth, long cast results. Double-taper lines have a short taper at the front and back, but the rest of the line is relatively large in diameter. If you are interested in just long-distance casting using full fly lines, these do the best job. They do have drawbacks for many fishing situations, so most fly fishermen prefer the longer tapered lines for a combination of distance and fishing.

Tournament casters early in the 1900s determined that shooting tapers were the easy path to distance casting. More commonly called shooting heads, they are relatively short, heavy sections of line (floating, intermediate, or fast-sinking line) attached to a super-thin line. If you false-cast only the head and release it, the heavy head will carry the thin shooting line a greater distance. During false-casting, a small amount of the thin running line is outside the rod tip. The distance from the rear of the shooting head to the rod tip is called overhang. If too much of the thin shooting line is outside the rod tip, then it can't support the unrolling loop. Some floating weight-forward lines have a short, heavy head section and the rear of the line is thin. This allows the angler to false-cast the relatively heavy, short head (such as in bass bugging or saltwater fishing) and then shoot to the target. The short, heavy section easily pulls the thinner running line to the target, obtaining the desired distance on the cast. Such lines, when measured from the front end to the end of the back taper, will rarely exceed 45 feet, and the remainder of the line is thin. Lines of this design are not the best for casting distance because the extra-thin line at the rod tip cannot support the loop of heavier line, and it will tend to collapse and create shock waves in the line, reducing possible distance.

The Stop

Remember that the casting stroke is comprised of a relatively long and continuous acceleration followed by a quick speed-up-and-stop. The acceleration causes the line to travel much faster, and the faster the acceleration, the greater the line speed. If the rod stroke is short, only the upper portion of the rod bends, but the longer the acceleration, the greater the line speed and the more the rod bends, so additional energy is stored for the final moment of the cast. Once the rod straightens on the speed-up-and-stop, the line will go in that direction.

This stop is critical to distance casting, which is why stronger people can cast distances over 100 feet. They have the muscles to rapidly accelerate and stop a rod. If you haven't before, try throwing an apple or potato off a stick. If you just come forward and throw it easily, the potato doesn't go very far. If you come forward, and just at the last minute, accelerate fast and to a hard stop, the potato goes an incredible distance. Come forward and follow through on the stop, which most people do, and you take energy away from the cast.

One of the greatest mistakes in distance casting is that people, as soon as they stop the rod, continue dropping the rod toward the water, which takes energy out of the cast. A good way to prove to yourself that this is not a good idea is to select a certain amount of line and throw two identical casts. As soon as you stop on the first cast, lower the rod tip; you'll find you open the loop and drag line toward the water. On the second cast, stop the rod and count out loud, "one, two, three," before lowering the rod. The loop will travel to the target much faster and tighter.

Tight Loops

Loop size is critical for distance. The most efficient cast unrolls the line directly away from the target and then back toward it. Large loops steal distance and efficiency in three ways. A large loop directs the cast's energy around a curve instead of at the target. Large loops need to be held up, and the energy to support that upright loop could have been better used to help the loop get toward the target. Large loops also have to penetrate more air. On a calm day most anglers think this isn't a problem—but wind is just air that blows toward you.

Loop size is determined at the end of the cast. Back and forward casts are the same; they just go in different directions. I will discuss the forward cast because many think it is easier to visualize. Once the rod bends as it sweeps forward, the line is aimed directly at the tip—with no sag. The rod hand may be moving forward in a straight line or plane, but it really is the base or pivot as the rod sweeps forward. The rod tip is not moving straight ahead but travel-

ing in a slight arc. After the line has been accelerated forward, if the speed-up-and-stop is very brief (remember that the tip is traveling in a minor curve or arc), then it drops slightly below the oncoming line. With a longer speed-up-and-stop, the rod drops lower than the oncoming line and a larger loop results. The more wrist movement in the speed-up-and-stop, the more likely you'll create a larger loop.

Aerializing Line

The amount of line you false-cast plays a role in how far you cast. If you want to cast 90 feet and false-cast 40 feet of line, the energy of the cast has to drag 50 feet through the guides to the target—not likely. But if you false-cast 60 feet of line, the rod loads deeply because of the increased weight and you only need to shoot 30 feet of line. To pick up a lot of line, the key is to not make the backcast until the line end leaves the water. If any line remains, you have to use energy to pull the line free from the surface tension. Many try to take the rod back at a near-vertical angle. At this angle you can't bring the rod far back behind you, so you don't have a wide range of motion to lift a lot of line from the surface. Because of this limited stroke, many anglers simply begin the backcast while the line is still on the water, or allow the rod tip to travel down and back during the speed-up-and-stop, creating a large loop and often deep sag in the line, affecting the efficiency of the forward cast.

To make a desirable, fast, flat backcast when picking up a long line, the rod tip must speed-up-and-stop while it is rising—and all line should be free of the water (not the leader—just the line). If you are facing the target, when the rod gets at a right angle to the target, the tip of the rod needs to be below your head.

There are two advantages to this movement. By moving the rod sideways, you can take it much farther back than in a vertical position. This permits

you to remove all the fly line from the surface. Also, if the rod tip is lower than your head when it passes beyond your body, it can still stop while rising, creating a flat, fast backcast. With this motion and a good double haul, you'll be able to get more distance.

Shooting Line

It's hard to pick up and cast the entire fly line, so you need to shoot line on your forward cast for a long-distance cast. To shoot a lot of line on a long cast, you need to carry more line in the air to deepen the bend in the rod. Even if you are a really good caster, if you have 35 feet of line outside your rod tip and you are trying to shoot to 90, two things are against you: You don't have enough weight to really bend that rod, even though you are accelerating very rapidly forward, and you are going to have to shoot almost 55 feet of line. If you want to make a longer cast, carry more line outside the rod so that you can bend the rod more deeply and have to shoot less line.

When you are retrieving line to make a cast, you need to have a certain amount of line out of your guides before you can shoot any amount of line, and the more line you have out, the more you can shoot. If you have 20 feet of line inside the guide and you are trying to shoot to 40 feet, you can't load the rod. As you make a normal backcast, haul fast and let the line flow through your thumb and fingertips, shooting line. Trap the line and begin the forward cast just as the line starts to slow down when it shoots through your hand. If necessary, sometimes you need to shoot line again on another backcast to get a lot of line out. Hauling is critical for this technique because you need enough line speed on the backcast so that you can drag line through the guides to increase the length of the backcast.

Many skilled casters also shoot line on their backcasts. One possible fishing situation where you'd need to

You can shoot line on both your back and forward casts. It is good practice to shoot line through your fingers for accuracy and to prevent tangles.

At the end of a forward cast, it is important to retain line control. You may be casting to a cruising fish that takes the fly as soon as it hits the water. If you are looking for the line to begin stripping, you may miss your opportunity to strike. Sometimes you realize that your forward cast is going wrong, and you can trap the line and make another false cast. You can also trap the line for accuracy by stopping the cast when the fly is over the target.

shoot line on the backcast is if you've stripped the fly line in and the fish follows your fly but then turns away. You only have a short amount of line to pick up, but you want to make a long cast, so you shoot some line on the backcast, make a forward cast, shooting line on the forward cast, shoot even more line on the backcast, and now you have enough line outside your rod tip to generate the mass necessary to carry the line to the fish.

Trajectory

When casting floating lines, you should stop the rod so that it is climbing slightly above your head. With weighted lines, which fall faster than floating lines, make your forward cast at a much higher angle than you naturally would, well above your head, which means a low backcast. If you make the speed-up-and-stop while the rod is slightly behind you, before your hand reaches your body, you can throw an elevated cast, which will unroll above your rod tip, and you can avoid hitting yourself in the head.

Cleaning Your Fly Line

To help anglers shoot more line, manufacturers add a lubricant to the lines so they will flow better through the guides. They do this in two ways. Some add a lubricant that is distributed throughout the line, and if some is removed from the surface, the lubricant has the ability to redistribute itself throughout the line. Other manufactur-

ers coat the line with a lubricant. It is important to know which process is used when cleaning lines. For the lines with internal lubricants, line manufacturers sell a scouring pad that can clean the line even if the line is wet. You fold the pad around the line, and draw the line through the pad (squeezing it against the line slightly) to remove the dirt. But such pads should not be used

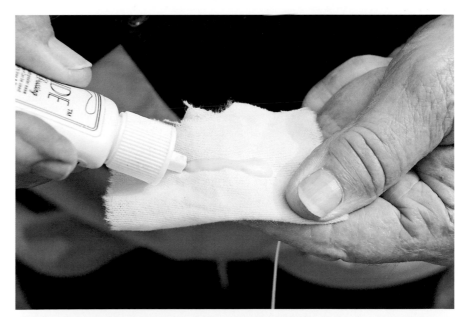

After cleaning your line, dress it with a lubricant such as Glide for the best results. Don't be frugal and use a product not designed for fly lines. Regardless of the line you use, one of the important factors in good line performance and casting farther is a clean line. Dirt and grit coating the line create undesirable friction as the line flows through the guides and can sink the tip of a floating fly line.

with line that is coated with lubricant, since the pad can scour away part of the lubricant. Contact the manufacturer of your line to find out what they recommend for cleaning.

Manufacturers also offer different materials you can apply to fly lines to make them slicker and shoot better. I recommend sticking with products designed for fly lines. Anglers have tried all sorts of home remedies, including Armor All, which is a vinyl cleaner used mainly to clean and refurbish vinyl in automobiles. It is a cleaner, so it will remove the lubricant on the outside of a fly line. If you apply it too often, it can reduce the effective amount of lubricant on or in the line. Armor All is also water-soluble. When it is first applied, the line is super-slick and shoots well. The slickness disappears soon after fishing simply because water washed it off the line.

There is one safe cleaning method for all fly lines. Fill a container with warm water and add a few drops of soap. Detergent may remove some of the line's lubricant, so make sure it says "soap" on the label. Immerse the fly line in the warm, soapy water and then scour it clean with a piece of terry cloth or old towel. Once the line has been cleaned, place it in clear water, and with a new piece of cloth, scrub it thoroughly to remove all soap. Any soap residue left will cause a floating line to sink.

Drifting

Advanced casters can combine a really good stop with some drift, continuing to move the rod tip back after the stop, to get the maximum rod loading. The longer you can move the rod, the longer you can store energy to create higher line speed. Drifting allows the caster to accelerate the rod over a longer distance, but I think it is best for beginners to learn to stop the rod where they want to go and become proficient at that before experimenting with the drifting technique. On some of my longer casts, I stop the rod dead,

but then I continue to extend my arm back after giving the line a chance to clear the rod tip.

To drift properly, you have to learn to wait long enough after the stop to allow the loop to escape the tip so that you don't pull it down, which takes a lot of practice. Once the loop gets 10 feet or so beyond the rod, you can drift back and not affect the direction of the cast or the size of the loop. You also have to elevate the hand and arm to drift properly, and you start to get into rotator cuff problems.

At times, you can also drift on the forward cast. If you need to work more line out and you want to make a long cast, pick the line up and shoot some line on the backcast. Then when you shoot line on the forward cast, if you extend the arm and rod forward at the end of that cast, you are drifting on the forward cast, and lengthening your casting stroke. This gives you more line speed on the backcast, which allows you to shoot even more line.

Long Overhead Cast

This is the most popular method of making a long cast. The rod moves a short distance before the backcast is made. It requires a good bit of power to throw a long backcast. This method makes it difficult to make long casts if you are not strong. This technique also involves flexing the wrist, and by elevating the elbow off the shelf, the rotator cuffs are stressed in both the back and forward casts. I can't flex my wrist as much as I used to be able to do—

when I cast in this manner when I was younger, I would bend my wrist during the drift so that the rod was almost parallel to the water.

Hold the rod low to start the cast.

Raise the rod vertically to begin drawing on the line. Continue to lift the line. A common mistake when making any backcast with a long line is to begin the backcast before the end of the line leaves the water. If some of the line is on the water when you make the backcast, you have to rip it free of surface tension, which takes energy away from the backcast and may produce shock waves in the line.

The moment you lift the line end from the water, make the backcast. Hauling on the backcast helps develop enough line speed to make a straight backcast without sag.

At the end of the single haul, my line hand is well away from the rod butt. If the hand remains there, two problems can occur. One, on the forward cast the line will frequently tangle in the reel or rod butt. Two, as the rod hand moves forward, it pushes line slack between the rod butt and the distant hand, which must be removed before you can begin the forward cast.

As soon as you stop your haul hand, it should begin moving toward the rod butt. If you allow the line loop to unroll well away from the rod, your hand can drift to the rear, with the rod aiding the forward cast.

Just before the backcast line unrolls, your line hand should be close to the rod, as shown.

Here, my rod hand is close to and just in front of the rod butt—perfect position for an efficient haul. The entire time the rod is accelerating forward, your line hand should be hauling on the line.

When your rod hand speeds up and stops, your line hand should stop hauling at the same time. If your line hand continues to haul—as so many anglers do—the rod tip doesn't stop but directs some of the energy of the cast downward. How fast you stop after accelerating forward greatly influences how far the line will go.

Allow the line to unroll well away from the rod tip before lowering it. If you follow through with the tip immediately after the speed-up-and-stop, you divert energy from the cast. Begin lowering the rod. Just before the line completely unrolls, the rod tip should be in a fishing position.

Sidearm Cast

When you want to make a long cast, you need to extend your arm well behind you to lengthen the stroke. The longer the rod travels through the stroke, the more it helps the cast. Proper backcast is also critical. Most fly casters use a vertical cast to pick up a long line, but the short stroke length limits how much line they can lift from the water. As a result, almost all long pickups with a vertical stroke require the rod tip to pass to the rear of the angler before the backcast is made. To make a straight backcast, the rod should stop while it is rising. Once the

rod tip passes vertically beyond the angler, it is very difficult not to cause the tip to travel down and back on the speed-up-and-stop, creating a sag in the line. The extra force needed to pick up the long line causes the rod tip to dip even farther on the stop, creating a large sag in the backcast. This is evident even among many good fly casters. No forward cast is possible until that sag is removed.

The more line outside the rod tip before making the last cast, the greater the potential distance. Of course, at some point you can overload the rod

with too much line, but most casters don't load the rod enough. One way to extend line is by a series of false casts. However, if each false cast is not just right, the final cast suffers.

A better way is to first extend a long line on the water in front of you, but picking up all this line requires good hauling technique. If the rod tip starts low, it pulls against the line held by surface tension. The longer the stroke, the more the rod loads, attempting to free the line from the water. A much deeper bend develops from pulling against the water's tension than from false-casting in the air. Couple the rod stroke with the double haul to make extra-long casts.

It is less efficient if the rod is raised vertically for a long backcast (either false-casting or lifting line from the water). During a vertical stroke, the rod loads mostly in the tip, the weakest portion of the rod. Line can only be lifted from the water until the rod is vertical. With some line remaining on the water and forced to make the cast, many fly

fishermen then overpower the stroke, causing the tip to dip downward on the stop, producing a sag in the cast. To make a backcast without sag, the rod tip must stop while it is rising.

A much more efficient method of making an extra long cast is to position as much line on the water as the angler can lift for the backcast. The lower the tip at the beginning, the more line you can lift and the more likely you will

make the speed-up-and-stop while the tip is rising. With a side cast, the rod can continue to lift line until the rod tip is beyond your body. This loads the rod more deeply, which aids the longer cast. Start the side cast with the tip near the surface, so the rod is still rising when the line end exits the water, enabling a backcast with a flat, tight loop directing all energy away from the target.

Long Sidearm Cast

Start with the rod low to the water. To make the longest backcast stroke possible, lean forward, reaching out with your rod hand. Make sure to remove all slack from the line. This cast allows more use of the body and develops longer strokes back and forward that generate additional line speed during the extended acceleration and load the rod deeper, storing more energy for the final moment of the cast.

Continue bringing back the rod, keeping your arm on the shelf. The rod continues to load. Wait for the line to leave the water before beginning the backcast.

Begin a low backcast. Raise the rod rapidly to lift line from the surface and wait until all the line is out of the water before making the backcast. If some line remains on the water as the cast starts, the rod bends, pulling on the line held by surface tension. Then as the line leaps from the water, it causes a jolt to the rod, creating shock waves in the backcast.

Note in the photo how far the rod tip traveled back before I lifted the line from the water. During the side backcast, the tip should be lower than your head when the rod tip passes beyond your body. This allows the rod tip to stop while rising, creating a flat backcast. If the tip is above your head, there is a good chance the rod tip will stop while going down and back and develop a sag that must be removed before you make the forward cast. A fast haul during the time the rod is accelerating aids in a long backcast.

After the speed-up-and-stop, you can extend your arm to the rear and even lift it slightly from the imaginary shelf as the line travels back at an upward angle. As you extend your arm to the rear, shift your body weight to your rear foot. This body swivel helps lengthen the stroke. The line outside the tip is traveling straight and free of sag.

Just before the line unrolls, begin a forward cast. Haul fast as you accelerate the rod forward.

Keep your elbow on the imaginary shelf as your arm sweeps forward, loading the rod.

To obtain the maximum stroke length, delay the speed-up-and-stop until the rod is well forward and the tip stops in the direction the line is to travel.

The tight loop created by a very short and abrupt speed-up-and-stop indicates all of the energy of the cast has been directed toward the target.

You want a flat line when making a long cast.

Backcast Basics

Too many anglers concentrate only on making good forward casts. But making a good backcast is, in many ways, more important. The first main problem that I see with many backcasts is that anglers don't time it properly. During the backcast, if you wait until you feel the tug of the line, the line will be totally extended, and you'll begin the forward cast too late. If a hunter shoots at a flying duck, he aims at where the duck is going to be, not where the duck is when he pulls the trigger. Similarly you should begin the forward cast while the line loop resembles a candy cane, before it has straightened completely. If there is a popping sound when the forward cast begins, you started forward too quickly. If you wait until the line opens or tugs, the line is falling, developing slack before you can start moving the line forward.

The other big problem is a backcast with a sag in it. To avoid this problem, the tip should speed up and stop while it is rising. Anytime the rod tip travels downward during the speed-up-and-stop there will be a sag in the line. The angle at which the rod tip stops as it rises determines the backcast direction. No forward cast is possible until the rod motion removes the sag and begins moving the line end.

A good backcast is elevated and has high line speed, creating nice tight loops. Look at your backcast. Before any efficient forward cast can be made, the backcast must be aligned in the direction of the target.

Kneeling in Water

When making a backcast while wading deep or sitting down in a canoe, drift boat, or kayak, anglers commonly hit the water behind them on their backcast, which spoils the forward cast. This is usually caused by a sag in the backcast line or the line being directed toward the water. Some anglers partially solve the problem by using longer rods to help elevate the sag in the line and keep the line above the surface. But long rods are more tiring to repeatedly cast and unnecessary with good technique. The key to making a good backcast is to stop the fly rod while it is rising so there is no sag in the cast. To accomplish this, begin with the rod tip close to the water, and make a side cast. A good double haul is essential.

When the line end leaves the water, I make the backcast. The butt has passed a vertical position. I speed up and stop, but because the rod has passed beyond a vertical position, the tip stops going down instead of rising.

This creates a large unrolling loop and sag in the line. The line as it unrolls is falling toward the surface as the large loop slows.

The line continues to sag toward the water. The longer the line used in the backcast, the more line will contact the water before a forward cast starts. The line contacts the water as the forward cast begins. This makes it more difficult to make a good forward cast, especially with a weighted fly.

To prevent the line from hitting the water on the backcast, start with the rod tip close to the surface. Begin lifting the line with a side cast, keeping your elbow on the imaginary shelf. Elevating your elbow during the cast tends to drive the line down on the backcast. As you continue to lift the line with the rod, pivot your body to aid the cast. The moment the line leaves the surface, speed up and stop and cease hauling.

It is critical that the rod tip stops while it is rising.

This ensures the line will not be diverted downward and there will be no sag. With a short speed-up-and-stop, the loop is tight and the line devoid of sag.

Stretching the Fly Line

When you pull many fly lines from the reel, they retain the position in which they were stored on the reel—in tight coils. Stretch the line to remove these coils to improve your casting. Slip the line under your foot. Grasp the line on both sides about shoulder high and pull firmly with both hands, but not excessively hard. This method can be used in a boat or along the stream and doesn't harm the line as long as your shoe soles are clean and you use only enough force to stretch out the coils. Below, the coils have been removed between my hands. Continue the process until you have removed all the coils.

Stripping and Shooting Coils

When you are wading deep and need to cast a long line, it's easy to get a messy tangle or lose distance because of the line tension on the water. If you control the coils of line as you retrieve the fly, you can usually shoot it trouble-free. A stripping basket helps but many freshwater anglers avoid them.

There are other ways to accomplish controlling loose lines, but I have found this one offers several advantages over some. This method reduces the amount of line lying on the water, making it easier to shoot line better. If properly stored, the line rarely tangles on the shoot. And it permits the

angler to move to another position with the coils of loose line under control. Some people like to place coils in their clenched lips. But I don't recommend this method because of *Giardia* and the questionable water quality on many of the rivers we fish.

Grip the line with your line hand as you would in a normal retrieve. Retrieve about 10 feet of line, allowing it to fall on the water beside you.

Before retrieving more line, position it at the joint of your thumb and hand and hold it firmly there.

Retrieve about another 10 feet of line.

Place the line under the thumb and finger about an inch or so forward of the line you trapped earlier.

You should now have two big loops. Retrieve the final 10 feet of line.

Trap the line now under the forward end of the thumb.

You are now ready to make the back-cast. Keep the three loops apart by your fingers.

Make the backcast while firmly holding the three loops of line, preparing to let go one of the coils when you make your forward cast. Begin coming forward, accelerating and loading the rod while hauling.

Speed up and stop, forming a loop.

Shoot one of the coils on the forward cast.

As the coil continues to shoot out, trap the line and begin hauling for a backcast.

Begin the backcast, and at the same time begin hauling.

End your haul as you speed up and stop on the backcast, shooting the second coil.

Begin moving your line hand toward your rod hand to haul before the final presentation cast.

Keep accelerating forward to load the rod deeply.

Shoot the last coil and the remaining line after you stop the rod.

Sometimes extending your arm at the end helps the line shoot through the guides. The line tension on the water helps the coils shoot without tangling.

To shoot a lot of line, you need to generate a lot of line speed with a good haul. The line was traveling so fast through the guides on this cast that I could have shot an extra 10 or 15 feet if I'd had it coiled up.

Note: When making this cast, you can shoot all three coils with only one backcast by shooting all the line that you hold. But it is easier to learn if you make two backcasts.

CHAPTER 6

The Roll Cast

The basic roll cast is one of the most useful casts whether you are fishing in salt or fresh water. It comes in handy for a lot of things: I use the roll cast for making casts when there is little or no backcast room behind me, lifting sinking lines to the surface of the water before beginning my backcast, picking up a dry fly, and freeing snags from stumps and downed trees. Unfortunately, it is the one cast most often performed poorly, largely because most casting instructors teach it the wrong way.

Most fly fishermen perform this useful cast poorly, primarily because of a poor forward cast. They tend to aim the rod tip downward, rather than straight ahead, and make a large sweeping motion rather than a short speed-up-and-stop. Videos and books for years have taught us to make a roll cast by driving the rod over and downward, which means the line will roll over and downward and collapse in a pile in front of us. But even though we need to modify the backcast, we should make a normal forward cast

to ensure that the fly travels above the water and not down in front of us. There are reasons for changing the angle of the forward cast in a roll cast, but you should generally focus on coming through in a straight line.

In a good roll cast, you only modify the backcast. Make the forward cast like you would any other cast, accelerating to a stop and aiming at or slightly above eye level. Roll casts rely on the line sticking to the water to load your rod, but too much detracts from your cast.

Basic Roll Cast

Begin the cast with the rod tip near or at the surface. You must bring sinking lines to the surface before making the roll cast.

Slowly raise the rod, tilting it slightly away from your body. If you bring the rod back and do not tilt it, the forward cast often gets tangled. Continue to slowly raise the rod and draw the line end toward you. Lifting it too quickly will often create surface disturbance, alerting nearby fish. For a short cast, imagine you are sliding the line back on the surface.

Tip the rod tip back when the line end is no more than 10 feet from you. With a short cast, you must pause with the rod long enough so the line end stops moving. It can only be a heartbeat, but this lets surface tension grip the line so the rod has something to pull against. With an extended line, there is no need to stop since the weight of the line will load the rod—such as with the switch cast or long-distance roll cast.

Accclerate the rod hand forward, and wait until the last possible moment before making the speed-up-and-stop. During the entire forward cast, keep your elbow on the shelf, and your rod hand should move at a consistent height. This will direct all of the energy of the cast straight ahead.

This results in a normal forward cast with a tight loop. The shorter the speed-up-and-stop at the end of the stroke, the tighter the loop will be. For the tightest loops, do not make the final speed-up-and-stop until your rod hand is in front of your body.

When the line loop is well away from the rod tip, continue to lower the rod tip to the fishing position before the fly touches the water.

In this rear view, notice how the rod is angled to the side. In all roll casts, you should angle the rod tip slightly away from the body so the line drapes outward. If you bring the rod tip back vertically or tilt it inward on the forward cast, the line will tangle around the rod. With every roll cast, the D loop in the line should be positioned opposite the target of the forward cast.

After a brief pause, start accelerating forward toward the target. Continue accelerating the rod forward with your elbow on the shelf and your rod hand traveling straight ahead.

If you delay the speed-up-and-stop at the end of the cast until the last moment and your rod tip stops while going straight ahead, the tight loop aims all the cast's energy at the target.

Wait for the line to unroll. Start to drop your rod tip. Continue dropping the tip, timing it with the line unrolling. Near the end of the cast, lower the rod to a fishing position.

WATCH OUT FOR: High Elbow, Breaking Wrist

The roll cast that I first learned—and the one that I see many anglers making today—does the opposite of all these things. My elbow is elevated off the shelf, and my wrist is bent.

I start the forward roll cast by flexing my wrist forward while dropping my hand and elbow and making a long sweeping motion of the rod, which produces a large, rounded line loop.

The rod stops while moving downward, creating a large, inefficient loop.

This results in wasted energy that doesn't go toward the target. Stopping the rod tip in a downward motion causes the front of the line and leader to be aimed at the surface short of the target area. Note that a portion of the front of the line lies in a crumpled heap on the water.

Improved Roll Cast

To make the most efficient roll cast, bring the rod and rod hand back as far as you possibly can for the existing fishing conditions so you can use the rod to help you make the cast. The farther you take the rod to the rear, the more it will aid in making the cast—this is the fourth casting principle. Extending your rod tip way back is good in some situations where you have overhanging canopy that would prevent you from bringing your rod straight up and back in a conventional roll cast. With this cast, you can extend your rod tip back and relatively low to avoid hitting your rod tip on tree limbs and other streamside obstructions.

After a brief pause to allow surface tension to grip the line and help load the rod, bring your rod hand forward, keeping it at the same height throughout the forward cast. If the tip stops in a downward direction, some of the line will be thrown downward. If the rod tips stops in the direction of the target, the line will go in that direction.

To get a nice tight loop, accelerate your rod hand forward but do not make the short speed-up-and-stop until your rod hand is in front of your body. Beginning the speed-up-and-stop before this results in a wide, wasted loop. If your elbow rises off the shelf, then the loop will enlarge, wasting energy. Keeping your rod hand and elbow

moving directly toward the target will ensure all the energy goes toward the target—as would any good forward cast. Most people who use this technique and still have some trouble start the speed-up-and-stop when their hands are either slightly behind or even with their bodies—and that means they are going to make a longer speed-up-and-stop, so the tip of the rod, which is not traveling straight (even though the hand is because it is pivoting), is going to throw a bigger loop in the line than we want.

Improved Roll Cast

Begin with the rod tip close to the surface. Lift the rod slowly with the rod tip angled to the side. Keep your elbow on the imaginary shelf and your rod hand well below your shoulder.

Continue to bring the rod back, drawing the line end closer. Make sure your elbow stays on the shelf and your rod hand is well below your shoulder. Continue to move the rod well behind you as far as the fishing conditions allow. Your line hand should follow the rod as it is being lifted. If your line hand remained motionless during the lifting, there would be a space between the two hands, and on the forward cast slack would result at first, spoiling the cast.

Extend your rod arm as far back as it can go in the existing fishing conditions.

For an ideal forward roll cast, the rod should be positioned well back, with your elbow on the shelf and your rod hand low. With roll casts less than 25 feet, the line end resting on the surface can be less than but no more than a rod length in front of you, as shown here. This is just enough line on the water to load the rod, but there is no extra line that must be torn free of the water before making the cast.

Don't delay beginning the forward cast, as the D loop will develop slack. Keep your elbow on the shelf, maintaining your rod hand at the same height throughout the forward cast to direct all the energy of the cast toward the target. If your hand travels up and down, the line will do the same. If your hand drops on the forward cast, it will cause the line end and leader to pile up. The longer the desired cast, the longer the forward acceleration.

Remember, the shorter the speed-up-and-stop, the tighter the loop. After accelerating, bring the rod to a quick speed-up-and-stop to form a small loop just as in a normal forward cast. If the rod tip stops while going downward, the line will go in that direction and can end up in a pile on the surface. Stop the rod tip in the direction you would for a normal forward cast to get a loop like this one.

If the forward roll cast is made properly, it should resemble a good forward cast with a tight loop, and the line from the rod tip to the unrolling loop should be parallel with the water and not have a deep sag.

Roll Cast Pickup

You should never pick up a dry fly or a popping bug until all the line is off the water. If you rip line free of the surface of the water, you can make a lot of splash that alerts fish. The roll cast pickup lifts the line more or less vertically from the water and doesn't spook fish. This cast also flushes more water from the fly and line, reducing spray when you make a forward cast. In trout fishing, one of the places that the roll cast pickup works very well is in the tail of a pool. If you are fishing a dry fly and the line is drifting back and

might be swept over the edge of a pool into the next pool, making a quick roll pickup lifts the fly almost vertically, without making a lot of noise. You can't make a conventional pickup because you tend to be raising your rod tip as the fly drifts back toward you. The roll cast pickup also works well on calm pools to quietly lift the line, leader, and fly without alarming wise fish.

Popping bugs can make loud fish-alerting noises when lifted for a backcast. If you pick some cupped-face popping bugs or deer-hair flies such as

the Letort Hopper off the water in the conventional manner, the line that is still on the water tends to pull them forward instead of up and creates disturbance on the water. The roll cast pickup lifts the fly vertically out of the water, eliminating this problem.

Roll Cast Pickup

Start a normal roll cast. When the line end is within 10 feet, stop drawing the rod and line back.

Accelerate the rod and make a high forward cast. Keep your elbow on the shelf and your rod hand low. In the final moment of the cast, speed up and stop the tip to get a climbing cast. The shorter and faster the speed-up-and-stop, the tighter the loop and the more efficient the cast. When you speed up and stop the tip, do not lower the rod. The unrolling line loop will begin to pull the leader and fly vertically from the water.

As the line unrolls, it continues to lift the leader and fly. The unrolling line will begin to straighten the leader. Once the fly is above the surface, you can make a backcast without creating a lot of disturbance on the surface of the water.

The moment the leader unrolls, begin the backcast.

During the backcast, your elbow remains on the imaginary shelf and your rod hand travels back in a level plane.

At the end of the backcast, begin a normal forward cast.

Switch Cast

This is an extra-long roll cast developed by Spey casters using two-handed fly rods. But like so many other Spey casts, this one works well with a one-handed fly rod, too. When making this cast, pay attention to the amount of line on the water before you make the forward cast. Spey casters call this the anchor. You only need as much line on the water as is necessary to load the rod. The perfect switch cast is when almost all the line is behind you and just the tip of the line anchors near where you are standing.

Unlike with short roll casts where the line should pause on the surface to load the rod, the extended line weight in the switch cast does not require pausing, and in fact you shouldn't pause, as the D loop may start to droop, creating slack. Because you pick up and drop a long line near you, it is advisable to haul on both the back and the forward casts.

The longer the roll cast required, the more line should be on the water in front of you. Begin with the rod tip close to the surface.

Lift the rod fairly rapidly while tilting it slightly away from your body. If you lift it too fast, you may create too much disturbance on the surface that could frighten nearby fish. Lift too slowly and a sag occurs in the line that makes it difficult to complete the cast.

Watch the line end. When it leaves the water, make the backcast.

The goal is to deposit the line on the surface of the water no more than 10 feet in front of or behind you. To accomplish this, angle the rod and make a short, side, circular motion with the tip. If the circular rod tip motion is made properly, the line end will fall close to you. Only practice will teach you how to position the line end correctly.

As soon as the line falls to the surface and stops, begin the forward cast. Don't pause too long or the D loop may begin collapsing, and you'll have to remove that slack.

Keep your elbow on the imaginary shelf, and accelerate your rod hand straight ahead. Note that your elbow and rod hand have been kept low. If you briefly speed up and stop in the direction of the target during the final moment of the cast, a tight loop is formed that delivers all the energy to the target.

When the rod tip stops, do not lower the rod immediately, or the loop will be opened and energy directed downward, detracting from the cast. When the line has unrolled well away from the rod tip, begin to lower the tip. Continue to lower the rod as the fly nears the target.

CHAPTER 7

Essential Fishing and Presentation Casts

I once knew one of the sorriest casters in the world. He would sweep the rod tip to the water, and his loops were 12 feet wide. But he would catch lots of trout. As he swept the rod tip down toward the water, the line and leader would stack up, and he could get incredible long drifts with his fly before drag set in. His poor casting technique turned out to be excellent fishing form. Better casters, who know how to stop the rod and let the line unroll, tend to pull out all the slack.

I am not telling you this to discourage you from becoming a better caster but to encourage you to learn how to make both controlled tight loop casts and controlled slack line casts. You may be able to catch a lot of fish with poor casting skills, but I guarantee you'll be able to catch a lot more if you improve your casting.

George Harvey showed me and thousands of other anglers that you need to have slack in front of the fly to make good drag-free drifts. He taught tens of thousands of students during (and after) his tenure at Penn State and in his demos and presentations. Harvey developed an elaborate leader formula to help even beginners get the slack that they needed, but I have discovered over the years that if you know the fundamentals of casting, you can put the necessary curves in your line and leader without that formula. Though leader designs can be important, the most important factor

is not the leader, but the one who casts it. Trout then weren't as wise or sophisticated as they are today. George's lesson now is even more important. To present the fly so that it drifts naturally to the fish, you must have a wave or curve in the leader immediately in front of the fly. If the leader remains straight inches in front of the fly, moving currents will act on it.

Pick up a garden hose lying on the grass with slack in the hose immediately in front of the sprinkler. Start walking with the hose, and the moment the hose straightens in front of the sprinkler, you begin to drag it. In dry-fly fishing you won't get drag as long as there is slack in front of the fly. Your leader doesn't need to land in perfect S curves. On some technical streams, anglers use 17-foot leaders and long tippets that fall in messes, but all that slack allows the flies to float perfectly.

Reach Cast

Trout expect food to be delivered in a natural manner and will almost always refuse a dry fly that drags across the surface, unless it happens to be imitating a natural that is also skittering. The single most important factor for successful dry-fly fishing is the ability to make a cast that presents the fly drag-free and naturally to the trout. When fishing across the current, anytime the fly line drifts downstream from the fly, the belly in the line will begin dragging the fly. The reach cast presents all of the fly line and leader upstream of the dry fly, allowing for a longer drag-free drift.

While the reach cast is considered a freshwater casting technique, it can pay off in the salt. I used the reach cast in the salt one year in the Florida Keys. The falling tide in Waltz Key Channel was carrying with it a small crab hatch. These little crabs couldn't fight the swift tide so they drifted along in it, and a few permit were sipping down these morsels near the surface. Eventually I figured out that the permit wouldn't take the fly unless it was drifting drag-free, and the reach cast was the perfect way to make that happen.

Reach Cast

Begin the cast with some slack line in your hand. Make a soft, elevated forward cast toward the target. The reach cast is one cast where high line speed is not usually desirable. You must make the forward cast on the reach (and stack) cast as gently as possible. Because you need to place line upstream, if the line is traveling too fast on the forward cast, you won't have enough time to lay the line over. If you aim the line too low on the forward cast, you won't have enough time to place the line upstream.

The high, slow cast gives you time to lay the fly line upstream by tilting the rod over instantly after the speed-up-and-stop.

Feed slack into the cast as you continue to reach upstream. Allow the slack to flow through your cupped first finger and thumb so you have constant control of the line. Slack continues to feed into the cast as the rod nears a parallel position. This is an important part of an effective reach cast. It is also important to feed line as you reach upstream so that you don't pull slack out of the line when you reach.

As the cast ends, the line is well up-stream of the fly. The elevated cast helps stack waves in the leader as the fly falls to the surface, ensuring a drag-free drift. That slack that you fed has not affected the forward portion of the cast. All slack has been fed through your hand as the cast ends.

If you hold onto the line as you reach upstream, then the slack, instead of feeding from the line hand, must come from the far end of the line, which jerks the line, leader, and fly back and spoils your accuracy. By holding the line in my hand, I pulled the slack from the front of the line instead of feeding it from my hand.

Because no slack is being fed from my line hand, the rod begins to pull back the line and fly. This results in shortening the line and often straight-ening the front of the line and leader, spoiling a good drag-free drift. For a good cast, the slack must originate at the line hand.

Feeding Slack

Close up view of feeding slack during the reach mend. To make a good reach, you need to place some slack line upstream of the fly. Not only must you place the line upstream of the leader and fly, but you must make an accurate cast.

Stack Cast

This cast has been around for a long time and has been called many things, including the tower, pile, puddle, and parachute cast. Several casts deliver soft waves in the front of the line and the leader, but I think the most accurate (even at long distances) is the stack cast. When people make this cast, they traditionally start the forward cast with the rod fairly elevated, which makes it difficult to get a high trajectory without tailing the loop. Suppose you stood 15 feet back from a building, and you tried to throw the fly up the side of the building. If you make a conventional backcast, stopping at maybe two o'clock or two-thirty, you can't do it. If you take the rod low behind you and back, you can throw up along the wall. The low

side backcast really helps set you up for a high forward cast. The farther back you go with the rod, the higher you can throw the line.

I use this cast most of the time when I want a soft dry-fly presentation. Whenever I have overhead room and there is no stiff breeze, this is my preferred cast for getting lots of drag-free waves in front of the line and leader. I also combine this cast with a reach cast to get an incredibly long drift, which is particularly helpful on larger rivers. The high trajectory and slow speed give you plenty of time to reach way upstream. What too many people do with the reach cast is make it low and fast, and by the time they lay the rod over, the line is already in the water.

A stack cast angles the line even higher. The more slack that you want in the line, the higher the elevation of the forward cast should be, to give the line and leader time to pile up. If the rod remains elevated after the speed-up-and-stop, the line sagging back from the tip will pull most of the created waves from the leader. The key is to stop and drop. If you make this cast properly, it is a very gentle cast—you don't shock the rod at all, and line will fall in a perfectly straight line, unless there is a wind, in which case the roll dump I discuss in *Casting With Lefty Kreh* is often a better alternative. If you want to make this cast in a wind, you have to try and compensate for the direction that the wind is blowing.

Start with the rod tip low, and remove all slack from the line. With this cast, you have more control with a low side backcast. Extend a little more line than what is normally needed to reach the target since the waves placed in the line as it stacks will shorten the cast.

As soon as the line end leaves the water, make the low side backcast. As the backcast unrolls, the rod is low and well behind you, which makes an elevated forward cast easier.

Begin the forward cast low, and then aim it high. The cast should be a slow, soft one. If there is too much speed at the end of the cast, the line recoils and spoils the presentation. Make a gentle speed-up-and-stop, aiming it high, before your hand gets in front of your body. If your hand is well in front of you, a higher cast is more difficult.

Note that the rod has stopped almost in a vertical position, helping to make a towering cast. The higher the cast is aimed, the more waves will stack in the line and leader.

As soon as you make the speed-up-and-stop, immediately lower the rod. Follow the line with the rod tip as it falls.

If you don't lower the rod immediately, the sag in the line near the rod tip will drag most of the desired waves from the line and leader. It is important to lower the rod immediately after the stop on the forward cast.

The front of the line and leader are beginning to fall vertically. The waves continue to develop in the line and leader as the cast nears the end. At the end of the cast, much of the forward portion of the line and the leader have fallen to the water with small waves that will create a drag-free drift. You can combine this cast with a roll cast and a reach mend to cover lots of different situations on the water.

Tuck Cast

George Harvey, as far as I know, invented the tuck cast, which is a great example of how you can modify the basic fly cast to solve fly-casting problems. To make a good tuck cast, the fly must have some weight—it is very difficult to make tuck cast with a dry fly. If you cast with the line and leader fairly straight as the fly drifts downstream, the current tends to loft the fly so it doesn't sink deep enough. Harvey discovered that he could tuck the sinking fly back under the line at the end of the cast to create slack and sink the fly

faster. Because the fly is now downstream from a portion of the forward end of the line, the fly can sink until the current pulls all slack from the leader and line. This allows the fly to dive deeper before a retrieve begins. Most people think the tuck is a useful tool for nymphs only, but it is just as effective when fishing streamers to get them deeper in the water column during the drift or retrieve. The weighted fly and long leader coupled with high line speed cause the tuck, which is why it is almost impossible to make a good

tuck cast with a dry fly or a very short leader.

When you stop the rod just past vertical, the weighted fly is going so fast that it ducks down, but the tip of the rod snapping back causes the tuck. To get the maximum tuck, overcast your target, stopping the rod tip high enough so that the leader and fly have enough time to duck under the line. Many anglers, besides not stopping the rod tip sharply enough, cast too low on the forward cast and do not give the leader and fly time to duck under the line.

Start with the rod tip at the surface and make a normal overhead backcast. (You can also make a sidearm backcast.) Allow the line to almost unroll.

Make a high cast that will allow the leader and fly to sweep under the fly line after you stop the rod on the forward cast,

The more vertically the rod speeds up and stops, the greater the potential for a good tuck. If the line is aimed low to the water, there is no room for the fly to tuck under.

The cast goes well beyond the target. As the line unrolls and the weighted fly sweeps forward, the rod tip flexes downward. At this point, don't lower the rod. Stop the rod dead to allow the tip to flip the tuck into the cast. When the rod tip flexes back, it jerks the weighted fly back, tucking it and the leader underneath the line as it all falls to the surface.

The tip has flipped back and begins tugging the fly and leader back.

The leader and line are falling vertically. If you need more tuck, make a faster forward cast. Because the cast was high, the leader and fly fall to the water well before the main fly line. As the line hits the water, there is a lot of slack in the leader. The fly continues to sink deeply because the slack in the leader isn't pulled out by the fly line.

Front view. The higher you stop the rod, the greater the tuck.

Curve Casts

A curve cast is just a tuck cast turned on its side, so many of the same principles that apply to the tuck apply to the curve. It works best with weighted flies and longish leaders, and the faster you bring the rod to a stop, and the heavier the weight on the leader, the more the line curves. You can throw a curve in the line pretty well with a dry fly, as long as the leader is short. There are two kinds of curve casts: sidearm and vertical. The easiest one to master is the sidearm curve, where you face the target and sweep the rod parallel to the water. The vertical curve is a challenging one but useful in some special situations.

You don't want to attack fish with flies; you want to swim your fly away from the fish as if it was a fleeing baitfish. If the fish is looking away from you, a cast allows the fly to swim from one side across a fish's field of vision.

If the fish is facing you, a curve cast allows you to retrieve the fly from one side to the other before making a turn toward you. Curve casts can be used to strategically lure the fish toward the fly but not toward the boat, which will spook it. Anytime you have a fish facing you—trout, bonefish, redfish, whatever—and you throw straight at the fish in the conventional manner, you draw the fish toward you, where it will eventually see the boat and spook. If you make a curve cast that swims the fly broadside to the fish, the fish will very often follow the fly, which is swimming away from it, and not see the boat.

Another great place for a curve cast is when you are fishing to laid-up tarpon, which on calm days or early in the morning suspend in the water with their dorsal or tail fins just sticking out of the water. If you throw a fly out in front of the fish and retrieve it, even a little 2-

inch fly will spook a hundred-pound tarpon. But if you make a curve cast from behind the fish and then swim the fly across the front of the fish, you get a more natural presentation.

I have since found many uses for this cast in fresh water. For trout, you can use a curve cast to swim a fly along a streambank or riverbank rather than throwing the streamer at the bank and pulling it back toward them. The fish only sees the back end of the fly rather than its profile. Cast with a downstream curve tight to the bank, and you can strip your fly along the bank for a longer time.

Bass often lie behind rocks and stumps. With a curve cast, you can cast a popper so that it hooks behind the rock or stump, and begin your retrieve. Sometimes you can't even see your fly, but rises are often audible and let you know when to set the hook.

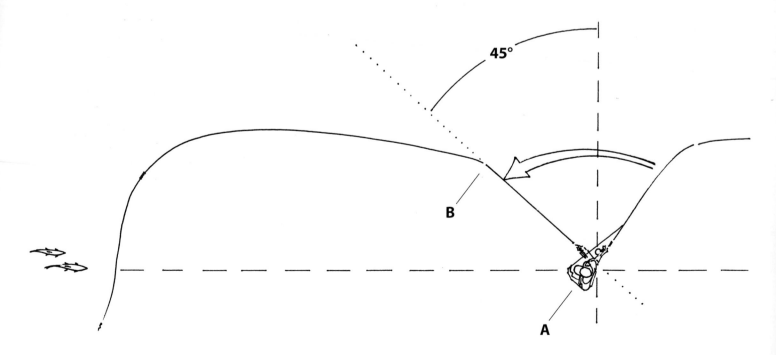

To be consistently accurate with the curve cast, you must first face the target (A). Then make a sidearm cast parallel to the water's surface, and stop the rod when the tip is 45 degrees to the target (B).

Sidearm Curve to the Left

The sidearm curve to the left is the easiest curve for a right-handed caster to master. Begin with the rod low to the side and close to the water. Move the rod back to begin lifting line from the water. Make a low, climbing back-cast. Just before the line unrolls, begin the forward cast. Keep the rod at a lowered angle on the forward cast (parallel to the water). To make accurate sidearm curve casts, it is important to face the target.

On the forward cast when the rod is 45 degrees from the target, make an extra-fast speed-up-and-stop with the rod parallel to the water. The faster the rod tip speeds up and stops on the forward cast, the greater the curve will be. Hauling and accelerating faster will produce a larger curve in the line.

If the curve is to travel parallel to the surface, the rod tip during the speed-up-and-stop must travel parallel to the surface. Many have trouble with the curve because they start the forward cast with the rod too high and tend to bring the rod downward on the speed-up-and-stop, resulting in little or no curve. Visualize the tip traveling slightly upward during the speed-up-and-stop,

After the speed-up-and-stop, slowly lower the rod tip. The high-speed stop, coupled with the weight of the fly, flexes the rod tip to the left, and your line, leader, and fly all go in that direction.

The fly and leader curve to the left. The faster (not harder) you move the rod tip during the speed-up-and-stop, the greater the curve.

Snap T

The snap T is a Spey cast especially helpful for trout fishermen using one-handed rods when the line and fly have drifted downstream and need to be repositioned upstream. Many fly fishermen have difficulty making the change of direction with weighted streamers and nymphs. The snap T makes it easy.

The word "snap" may convey a violent rod motion, but the casting strokes are rather gentle. The cast is illustrated by a right-hander.

Lower the rod near the surface, allowing the line and leader to straighten downstream.

Raise the rod slowly at first so the rod tip travels as if it is inside an imaginary wheel. Just before the rod gets to this position accelerate the rod tip so it lifts the line from the water.

When the rod tip is opposite the target, sweep the rod down and slightly toward the line downstream. This will cause the line and fly to travel upstream.

Allow the line to fall to the surface—you will need that tension to help load the rod.

Lower the rod tip and sweep the rod around, stopping in the direction of the forward cast.

Make a backcast opposite the target.

Allow the line to properly unroll behind.

Begin the forward cast.

An easy, gentle change of direction has been made.

Change-of-Direction Cast

One of the most common situations where you need to make a change-of-direction cast is after the line drifts downstream and you want to cast it quickly back upstream. Or you may be fishing to a feeding trout when suddenly one rises in another direction. Many Spey casts are designed to make similar changes of direction, but this one only requires knowing the basic casting motions and can help those who might not know or might not want to use Spey casts. I use this for short casts (15–20 feet), and for longer casts I usually use a variation of the snake roll, which I cover in *Casting with Lefty Kreh.*

The key to this cast is to keep sweeping the rod along the surface until it points at the target. You must keep the rod tip as close to the water as possible and fight the tendency to elevate the rod. By keeping the rod tip as close to the water as possible, you maximize the length of the backcast stroke.

Lower the rod to within inches of the surface.

Sweep the rod upstream, close to the water. Continue sweeping the rod in the direction of the cast while beginning to turn so you will be facing the target.

Keep sweeping the rod along the surface of the water until it points at the target. By keeping the tip as close to the surface as possible, you maximize the length of the backcast stroke. You should now be facing the target. Without pausing after the sweep of the rod, make a slightly rounded motion of the rod tip and then accelerate directly away from the target. A short haul on the line helps. Do not elevate your elbow (a common mistake), as this will open the line loop.

Speed-up-and-stop directly away from the target. The backcast will flow opposite the target.

Wait for the line to unroll behind you. Just before the line unrolls on the backcast, begin the forward cast. Keep your elbow on the shelf throughout this cast. Speed up and stop the rod toward the target.

It is best to face the target before making the forward cast.

Make a normal forward cast toward the target.

Low-Side-Up Cast

Most fly rods are 8 to 9 feet long, and if you make an overhead cast, the line is traveling more than 10 feet above the surface. It's easy to alert fish in shallow or calm water, and with the overhead cast, if the unrolling line doesn't spook the fish, it most certainly will when it hits the water. The low-side-up cast keeps the fly line close to the surface and unseen. At the end of the cast, the leader and fly are directed upward. This expends all the energy

and deposits the fly as if it parachuted down to the surface.

I first started using this cast for bonefish in the Florida Keys many years ago. The best fishing can be when the sun is high overhead, enabling you to see the fish. But this also makes it easier for fish to see you and the fly line. On a really calm day, problems compound because not only are the fish going to see the fly line with a conventional cast, but there is no chop on the

water to mask the disturbance of the line and fly when they hit the water. If you cast with a normal overhead cast using a weighted bonefish fly, it is hard to get a relatively delicate presentation.

On calm pools in a trout stream, it's more often than not the line falling to the water that scares the fish. If you make a low-side-up cast, the fish is never going to see the line because it is going to be so close to the water, and the linc is only going to fall a short distance to the water, which lessens the impact. Most important, in a vertical cast the end of the fly line often whips forward. In fact, a fly that is too heavy will often duck under and tangle from the force. With a proper low-side-up cast, the leader and the very forward portion of the line go up at the end of the cast, which exhausts all the cast's energy. So in effect, you get the same results as if you went out there and just released the fly a few feet above the water. You get a much softer presentation, you hardly get any noise from the fly hitting the water, and you keep the line out of the fish's sight. Because of the soft presentation, this cast might be a better choice than a regular sidearm cast in very calm water—in a big trout pool or when fishing laid-up tarpon in glassy water.

This is a stealth cast. Crouch if you are close to the fish. Point the rod at the fish and carefully draw the line back. Continue drawing the line back close to the water.

When the line end leaves the water, make a low backcast. The low-side-up cast is more difficult to make from a high rod angle, and you are more likely to alert the fish.

Just before the line unrolls, begin the forward cast. In the beginning, the forward cast should be close to the surface.

As you accelerate the rod to just in front of your body, speed up and stop, going parallel to the surface but finishing upward. The rod and unrolling line come forward close to the surface, unseen by the fish. If made correctly, your thumb will point up on the stop. Study the photos above to see how your rod hand must speed up and stop upward. If the cast ends with your thumb on the stop parallel to the water, a basic side cast results.

Most of the line is within a foot or two of the surface as it is falling, and the leader and fly have stopped going forward, exhausting the energy of the cast. Note the line is traveling low and unseen by the fish while the leader and fly are climbing.

The line has gently dropped to the surface, and the line end and the fly are settling softly to the water.

Speed Cast

When fishing for tarpon and bonefish, you often can't stand there and take 10 minutes to work out as much line as you need to cast to the fish. You are at the mercy of the fish. If you are poling along and all of a sudden a bonefish shows up, you need a plan.

You can't have all the line that you think you'll need stripped out ahead of time and dragging around in the water—it would get tangled up in the grass—and you can't have it on the boat deck where it would get blown around. The solution is a speed cast,

where you hold the fly in one hand to get the fly to a fish with as few false casts as possible. The basic speed cast is the easiest to learn, but it has limited range. The longer version is good for distances of 20 to 30 feet.

Extend about 10 feet of line outside the rod tip. Hold the line just behind the first stripping guide. The rod hand holds the rod and the fly. The thumb and finger hold the hook so the point is free and points away from you so you won't be impaled.

Wind on Casting Arm

Anglers working the beaches almost always have an inshore wind, as air from over the cooler seas moves toward the warmer land. Big-river fishermen seeking steelhead and salmon constantly battle wind, as do trout anglers fishing light lines on Western rivers. Many bonefish, tarpon, and redfish are lost because the wind blew the fly off target. Yet wind can be your friend. The wind ruffles the surface and disguises imperfect casts that on a calm surface would have spooked the fish. With a good wind at your back, you can cast more line than the store sold you.

When the wind is blowing toward your casting arm, it can blow the fly into you or tangle your cast. To prevent the line and fly from hitting you, make a sidearm cast, and as you come forward, tilt the rod to the downwind side of you. You don't need to tilt a lot, because the wind will blow the line and fly to the other side of you. Many anglers are taught to cast cross arm, but this restricts your casting motion, and you can't get any distance with this cast. If the wind is blowing really hard to your casting arm, turn around and present the fly on your backcast.

If the wind is blowing toward your rod hand, lower the rod and remove all slack. Make a sidearm cast with the rod traveling low on the backcast.

If you make a backcast well to the side, the wind cannot blow the line or fly at you.

Just before the speed-up-and-stop, make sure the rod is tilted slightly to the downwind side of you. On the speed-up-and-stop, direct the line slightly to your downwind side.

In a strong wind, you don't need to the tilt the rod. If you bring it forward vertically, the stiff breeze will carry the fly harmlessly to the downwind side. The line stays out of harm's way as it unrolls forward. The cast ends with no problem from the breeze.

CHAPTER 8

Casting Weight: Split Shot, Sinking Lines and Shooting Heads

Fly fishermen often complain about casting weighted lines, which can be a sinking tip, sinking head, or complete sinking line, and weighted flies. Some have so much trouble casting weight that they often refuse to use it, limiting what they can catch. Weighted lines and flies will let anglers reach fish that would otherwise never see their offerings.

When saltwater fly fishing, I would rather cast a lead-core shooting head than a floating line—there is so little effort required. Because of their thin diameter and weight, weighted lines load the rod better, cast heavier or more air-resistant flies, go a longer distance, and can be thrown more easily on windy days. When you cast a floating line and a fly of little weight, the line begins to slow near the end of the cast. The opposite occurs with weighted lines and flies. Once the weighted lines or flies are set in motion, they tend to continue in that direction. It is the abrupt change in direction from the back to forward cast that causes so many fly casters trouble with weighted lines and flies. When a trout fisherman is casting a long leader with a fly on the end, a dropper, a split shot, and an indicator, the abrupt change in direction from back to forward cast can make the leader tangle

badly. Learning to make a smooth transition from back to forward cast avoids those tangles.

It is necessary to avoid that quick change in direction by making a different backcast stroke. What is needed is for the line, leader, and fly to travel in a circular motion during the change from the backcast to the forward cast. The line goes in the direction in which the rod speeds up and stops. Be sure to start with the rod tip just above water level. During the backcast, keep the elbow on the shelf and the thumb behind the rod handle away from the target and imagine you are going to sweep the rod tip around the inside of a horseshoe sitting on one leg. The faster you sweep the line around the inside of the horseshoe the great the distance obtained. The backcast will be circular and resemble the inside of a horseshoe; there is no abrupt change in direction.

The other huge problem with these types of rigs is hitting yourself or hitting your rod with them. Once you get two-thirds of the way around the horseshoe, if your hand is behind your body, you can then elevate the cast so that it travels high above your head: You avoid hitting yourself and you avoid hitting your rod, which can be disastrous if you hit it with a heavily

weighted fly. On the forward cast, once your hand is even with the body or in front of it, then the backcast is being directed at you or your rod tip. Begin the forward cast farther behind you to avoid hitting yourself. If you make a low sidearm backcast, you can start the forward cast behind your body, which keeps everything away from your head.

When casting sinking lines, a lot of anglers have trouble with the end of the line dumping at the end of the cast. If they make a straight cast, the line dumps under in a pile, but even worse, if they twist their wrists at all, the line dumps and curves to the left or the right (think unintentional curve cast here) and ruins their accuracy. The rod should come forward vertically—over the top—for the most accurate cast. That should prevent any curving to one side or the other. To prevent any dumping, don't make the forward cast too fast. The backcast is what loads the rod; when you make the forward cast, just come through smoothly and gently. Also, you might try lengthening the leader a little bit. The leader acts like a tail on a kite and helps turn the line over better. The same thing applies when you are using floating lines with steep, heavy front tapers, such as saltwater or bass lines.

Water Haul or Lob Cast

This lob cast is the best way that I know of to easily cast weighted flies and leaders with split shot and indicators on them tangle-free. I often recommend that beginners use this cast to become comfortable casting multiple flies or nymphs with shot before moving on to the weighted line cast, also called the Belgian, or oval, cast. Weighted nymphs create casting problems because of the quick change in direction from back to forward cast. Anyone who fished minnows or hellgrammites on a fly rod years ago like I did soon discovered that a quick change of direction during casting meant losing the bait. The water haul allows you to change directions smoothly and eliminate problems like hitting yourself or your rod with the weighted fly or flies or tangling the leader. This sequence shows how to smoothly lift two weighted flies and make a smooth forward cast.

Two weighted nymphs have been fished through productive water and need to be recast for another drift. Because the nymphs are weighted, a conventional cast with a quick change of direction can cause problems. Lower the rod to remove slack.

Start the backcast with your thumb behind the target and do not twist your wrist. Cast a wide, slow loop to prevent tangles and follow through with the rod tip.

As soon as the backcast ends, lower the rod tip almost to the water, extend your arm to the rear, and shift your body weight back.

As soon as the fly touches down (don't let it sink), begin drawing the rod forward.

Don't rush the cast as you smoothly draw the rod forward. It will begin to load. There has been no abrupt change in direction.

Continue to smoothly move the rod forward. This will lift the line and fly from the water and load the rod. The two weighted flies are smoothly rising from the water as you begin the forward cast.

Aim the cast rather high so that the weighted flies will travel well above you.

As soon as the flies have passed in front of you, begin to lower the rod.

The water haul allows you to cast multiple flies (or leader with split shot) easily and without tangles.

Water Haul with Sinking Line

During the retrieve, a weighted fly or sinking line swims well down in the water column. You must roll cast the line and fly to the surface to make an easy backcast. Once the weighted line or fly is on the surface, water tension pulls against the line on the water, helping you to deepen the load in the rod. In the sequence shown here, I am casting a weighted shooting head.

On the backcast before the presentation cast, the line and fly should travel around a curve. If you speed up and stop in the same plane, the abrupt change of direction creates shock waves and tangles.

One of the most important things to focus on when making this cast is to begin the forward stroke well behind you so that you can speed up and stop going upward, while your rod hand is still slightly behind your body. This ensures that the fly will travel well above you.

Before making a backcast, roll cast the weighted fly line to the surface. Remove all slack from the line and lower the rod tip.

Raise the rod to lift the line until the end is free of the water. Keep your elbow on the shelf.

Retrieve enough line so that you can lift all the line from the surface. Once the line is out of the water, continue to bring the rod back, dragging the leader and fly to the surface. With the rod well behind and all the line, leader, and fly on the surface, you can make a roll cast—a single haul often helps. If the roll cast does not lay the line out straight, do it again.

As soon as the speed-up-and-stop directs the line and fly straight ahead, lower the rod to the surface. Note that I have shot a little bit of the running line through the guides, and there is a proper amount of overhang when I begin the backcast. Don't wait too long or the line or fly will sink below the surface, and it will be difficult to make the backcast.

A single haul helps. The lower the rod is drawn back, the easier it is to make the proper forward cast.

The moment the fly leaves the water, make a continuous, rounded speed-up-and-stop. The line and fly should travel around a curve on the backcast. To increase the line speed and rod loading, a fast, continuous single haul while the rod is accelerating will produce a longer cast, aiding in throwing heavier lines and flies. If enough speed is generated on the circular backcast, little effort is required to make a long and efficient forward cast.

Keep moving the rod in a continuous circular motion during the backcast. Speed up and stop upward while the rod hand is still slightly behind your body. This causes the fly to travel well above you and also prevents the fly from striking the rod tip.

This is one of the few casts where your elbow should be well above the shelf at the end of the cast. Because of the climbing angle of your forward cast, the line and fly pass well above your head. Shoot line through the guides as soon as you stop the rod. This method requires only one circular backcast when performed correctly.

You know that you have made a good cast when all the remaining line shoots through the guides and pulls tight.

Double Water Haul

This is a particularly helpful cast when two people are in a boat—it helps you avoid casting through the boat and hitting a companion. After roll casting the line to the surface as in the single haul, you want to flop the sinking line on the water behind you (just like in the lob cast on page 123).

When the end of the line leaves the water, speed up and stop, simultaneously making a single haul. If you have kept your thumb behind the handle and have not twisted your wrist, the line will travel in a straight line behind you. After you speed up and stop, lower the rod tip while the fly is in flight. The moment the fly and front of the line touch the water behind you, begin a long drawing motion with the rod until almost all the line is off the water, while hauling to begin the forward cast.

The surface tension gripping the line bends and loads the rod deeply. A climbing angle of flight is desirable for the line and fly, so let your elbow begin to rise from the shelf as your rod hand comes forward.

You want the heavy line (and possibly the attached fly) to travel well above you so it doesn't strike you or the rod. Speed up and stop going upward, immediately after the line end leaves the water and while your rod hand is slightly behind your body.

The angle of flight is roughly 45 degrees, causing the line and fly to travel well above you.

Just before the line unrolls, lower the rod to a fishing position. Keep your arm and rod elevated as all the running line shoots through the guides.

Overhang

A shooting taper (more commonly called a shooting head) has two parts: The forward portion or head can be a floating line, a fast-sinking line, or anything in between. The rear portion (commonly referred to as the shooting line) is a much thinner and lighter line. These lines can be separate and connected with a loop-to-loop connection, or they can be integrated into one fly line. Because the thinner shooting line offers so little resistance when going through the guides, the heavier head can travel great distances. When you're fishing with sinking heads, greater depths can be obtained with the fly because the shooting line offers less re-sistance to the water than a conventional fly line.

When you're casting, the amount of shooting line outside the rod tip is called overhang. Too little running line outside the rod tip limits distance. Too much running line outside the tip won't support the heavier head as it turns over to unroll toward the target. The ideal amount of overhang differs with each rod/line combination and angler. To determine the correct overhang is easy. Too much overhang, and you'll see shock waves in the line. Too little overhang, and you don't get maximum distance.

When getting used to a new line, false-cast it, starting with no overhang, and add a little more shooting line each false cast to test the limits of your tackle. When small shock waves appear, retract the shooting line until the waves disappear.

I don't know why this is, and perhaps someone can explain the physics to me sometime, but if you shoot a little extra line on your backcast (before the final presentation cast) and extend your overhang, you do not cause shock waves in the line and you can cast much farther. You effectively increase the amount of overhang for your forward cast—more than I would recommend picking up—but it doesn't cause shock waves.

Overhang

The orange line is the running line and the white line is the shooting head. About 7 feet of running line is outside the rod tip here as I raise the rod to lift line from the water. This is too much overhang for most casters.

After you begin the forward cast, the line at the rod tip must begin unrolling, pulling the rest of the line forward. The shooting line is so thin that it collapses under the weight of the heavy head. You have too much overhang when you see shock waves in the line as it unrolls forward of the tip. Shock waves create tangles in the line, tailing loops, and poor presentations.

For most anglers 1 to 3 feet is the best amount of overhang. Advanced casters can handle more. Lower the rod and re-move all slack from the line before lifting the line from the water.

Begin the forward cast just before the backcast unrolls. Hauling shortens the length of the overhang. The rod accelerates forward. Only a short amount of overhang is outside the tip, and the loop is smooth. Gradually work out more overhang until you see shock waves, and then shorten the overhang until they disappear; that is the right amount of overhang for you and your rod and line.

Managing Line

Stripping baskets are simply containers attached to your body into which you deposit retrieved line. Some baskets are meant to be worn in front, others at the side, and most can be repositioned depending on what is comfortable for you. I have always been more comfortable with a side stripping basket, but this is simply a matter of choice.

Most stripping baskets are held in place by a belt or elastic strap or band. I prefer a shoulder strap for a side basket and an adjustable strap that also secures it to the leg so that the basket stays in position, even if you have to run down the beach after breaking fish.

A stripping basket is useful for all kinds of fly fishing. Surf fishermen are plagued by line dropping into the suds and becoming a tangled mess. Many fish have eluded anglers in boats when the angler somehow stood on the line, or it caught on something in the boat, ruining the cast. Even trout fishermen who move along a stream dragging line behind them or having it snag in the grass can profit from using a basket.

Any trout fisherman who has cast from the back of a drift boat knows how many things can catch the line. In addition to preventing snags, baskets keep line cleaner by preventing it from getting underfoot on a dirty deck or, even worse, on a sandy beach.

There are several stripping basket designs, ranging from buckets (VLMD, vertical line management devices) that sit on the boat deck to baskets that you wear. There are even flat mats with fingers that hold the line dropped to the deck at the angler's feet. Some of the best designs are baskets that collapse or fold so they can be placed in a duffle bag and accompany the fly fisherman on a distant trip. I predict that more and more fly fishermen will see the value of these baskets and use them. All have a use, and you have the option of buying one manufactured for fly fishers or building your own.

When wading while fishing the flats for bonefish or permit and especially when freshwater trout fishing, you may only need a relatively short line, and a large stripping basket may be unnecessary. However, a basket can also come in handy to prevent grass from snagging your line when stalking trout along a weedy bank or when hiking from pool to pool. The basket that I like is called the Stalker (for information concerning it, contact Alu-Marine Corp., P.O. Box 1332, Islamorada, FL 33036).

Because baskets can get water in them from waves or when wading deep, I prefer a side basket with many relatively large drain holes. And *all* stripping baskets should have cones or other fingers to hold the retrieved line in place. In homemade baskets, many prefer to use cable ties for these fingers.

The VLMD is most useful when fishing from a boat. It does limit somewhat where and how you can move when casting, but it has many advantages. The height of the VLMD is critical. I like one where the upper edge is about even with my crotch.

Many fly fishermen prefer to place a little water in the bottom, believing that it allows the line to shoot with fewer tangles. Some VLMDs also have upright fingers in the bottom to hold the line in position as it is retrieved, reducing tangles on the cast.

For best results, add a little more line to the VLMD than you will cast. This permits the line to better fall into the VLMD as each retrieve begins. I prefer to keep the VLMD between my legs so that when retrieving I always know exactly where to drop line. If I change position, I simply pick up the VLMD and move it so it is between my legs in the new casting direction.

When moving from one location to another, the line need not be spooled back on the reel but can remain in the VLMD. Upon arriving at the next location, simply pick up the rod and start casting. These buckets improve your casts so much, some anglers take them with them on trips to ensure they have them even if their guides don't. If you have fished out of boats in other countries, the VLMD is a real blessing. Dan Blanton and I, as well as other anglers, store our gear and clothes for a trip in a VLMD and then place it in a bag with wheels and check it at the airport. Some very light, folding VLMDs can be carried in a duffle bag, and some anglers use the collapsible lawn and leaf buckets available in many home improvement stores.

Steve Kantner once took me to a street in Fort Lauderdale where a lot of grass carp lived in a canal bordering the street. The carp were feeding on berries falling from trees on the far side of the canal, so long casts were required, which often were spoiled when the line tangled in the grass at our feet. We went to Kmart and bought a large rectangular plastic box about 30 inches long, 16 inches wide, and 18 inches deep. We set it on the grass at our feet and stored the retrieved fly line in it and never had another ruined cast.

Cable ties in my Stalker basket hold the line in place when I am moving about but allow the line to flow freely on the cast. You put in the basket a little more line than is cast. That way, at the beginning of each retrieve, the line in the basket helps bring the retrieved line in, too. If you cast all the line each time, you then have to place the first part of the rear line in the basket. If you have some line remaining in the basket when the cast finishes, it helps feed the line into the basket better.

Index